The Quranic Ten Commandments

"This is My Straight Path"
Al An'am (6:153)

Volume II

Hussein M. Naguib, Ph.D.

The Quranic Ten Commandments
Volume II
Copyright © Hussein M. Naguib

ISBN-13: 978- 0692721599(Hussein M. Naguib)
ISBN-10: 0692721592

بِسْمِ ٱللَّهِ ٱلرَّحْمَٰنِ ٱلرَّحِيمِ

In the Name of Allah, Most Gracious,

Most Merciful

The Quranic Ten Commandments
By
Hussein M. Naguib

Abstract

Filling a gap in the current literature, the author presents the first detailed study in English on the Quranic ten commandments as depicted from Surah *Al An'am*, verses 6:151, 152 and 153. The study is presented in two volumes. Volume I* covered an introduction and the first five Quranic commandments; and volume II analyzed the last five commandments. The full meaning of each commandment is shown by studying the Quranic verses related to the subject, as well as the teachings of Prophet Muhammad (peace be upon him) and his companions.

With extensive research and careful selection of Quranic verses and reliable sources of Prophet Muhammad's traditions, this book would be beneficial to students and teachers of schools and academic institutions, religions comparative studies, Quranic study groups, interfaith group dialogues, as well as any Muslim or non-Muslim who is asking: "Is there anything in the Quran similar to the Ten Commandments in the Bible?

Volume I was published by Amazon.Com (2014)

Volume II
Table of Contents

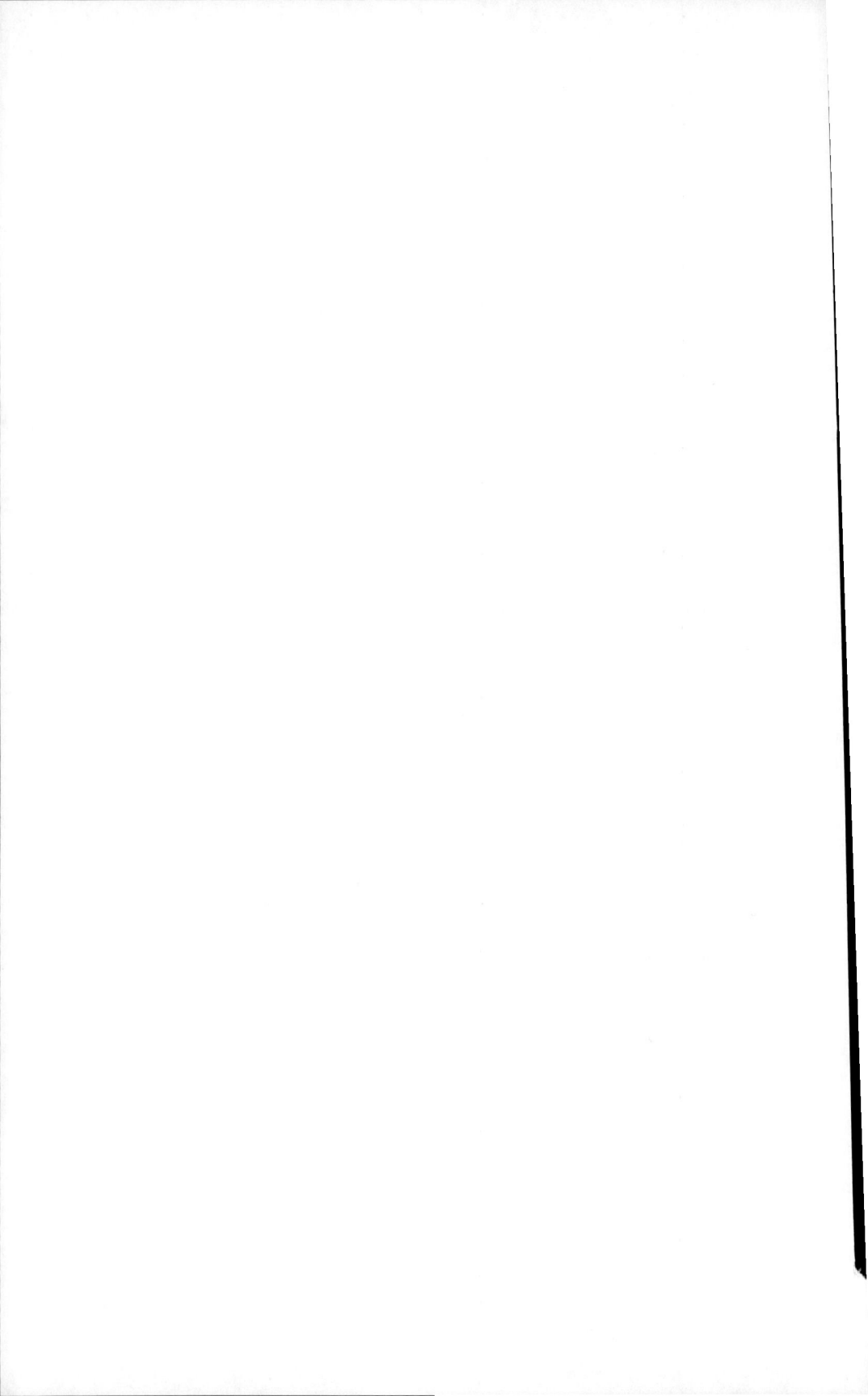

The Sixth Quranic Commandment
"Do not touch the orphan's property, except to improve it"

Meaning of the Words

In Arabic the sixth Quranic commandment from Surah *Al-An'am* (6:152) reads as follows:

وَلَا تَقْرَبُوا مَالَ الْيَتِيمِ إِلَّا بِالَّتِي هِيَ أَحْسَنُ حَتَّىٰ يَبْلُغَ أَشُدَّهُ

"Wa la taq'rabul- malal yateemi ella billati hya ahsan hatta yablogha ashoud'dahou"

Let us examine the English translation of each Arabic word in this statement:

"wa" means "and", which implies that this commandment is in addition to the previous five commandments; *"la"* means "no' or "not"; *"taq'rabu"* is the plural grammatical format of the verb *"eqtaraba"* means "come near"; *"mal"* means "money", "property", or "wealth"; *"al-yateem"* means the "orphan"; *"ella"* means "except"; *"billati hya ahsan"* means "with whichever is beneficial (to the child); *"hata"* means "until"; *"yablogha"* means "he reaches"; and *"ashoud'dahou"* means "his full strength".

Accordingly, the Quranic sixth commandment is translated as follow:

"And come not near to the orphan's property, except with whichever is beneficial to him, until he (or she) attains the age of full strength"

Other translations of the sixth Quranic commandment include the followings: *"come not nigh to the orphan's property, except to improve it, until he attains the age of full strength"* [1]; *"and do not even draw near to the property of the orphan in his minority except in the best manner"* [2]; *"And approach not the wealth of the orphan save with that which is better, till he reaches maturity"*[3]; *"and come not near to the orphan's property, except to improve it, until he (or she) attains the age of full strength"* [4]; *"and do not touch the substance of an orphan-save to improve it-before he comes of age"*

[5]; and *"Do not touch the property of an orphan before he comes of age, except to improve it"* [6].

More detailed analysis on the meaning of the words in the sixth commandment is presented in the following sections.

The Orphan

Definition

The Arabic word for "orphan" is *"yateem"* (Pl. *"yatama"* or *"aytam"*). The linguistic meaning of orphan is simply "one that is singular and alone". In Islamic Law, it means: "a child, male or female, whose father dies before the child reaches puberty" [7 - 10]; these children are classified as "true orphans".

There is another class of orphans called "virtual or implicit orphans" (*Yateem Hukmy*) which is defined by the Muslim Jurists as those children who lost their father's guardianship through various circumstances other than death. These cases include the following:

- The child whose father disappeared and nobody know whether he is dead or alive (*awlad al mafqoud*).
- The child who is abandoned by, or deserted by his parents (*al laqeet*).
- The child of a divorced mother who became incapable of caring for her children due to the lack of support from her ex-husband, or due to poverty or sickness (*awlad al motalaqueen*).
- The child of a prisoner or a detainee (*awlad al asra*)
- The child who lives on the city's streets escaping from maltreatments and/or exploitation by his or her own parents or step parents (*awlad al shawari'e*).

In these cases, the child will have the same rights and care of a true orphan i.e. the one whose father died.

Orphans' Rights

Based on Islamic and universal standards, all children, including orphans, have the following rights:

- The right to grow up in a nurturing, loving environment where their physiological, psychological, and intellectual rights are met.
- The right to know their lineage, and to celebrate their unique national, cultural, linguistic, and spiritual identity.
- The right to have a safe, supportive environment where their rights to dignity, education, and the development of their talents are well respected.
- The best interest of the child should be the primary consideration in all decisions related to children.

Orphans Prevalence and Statistics

Worldwide Data [11]

- A 2005 UNICEF report has estimated that there are between 143 million and 210 million orphans worldwide. This estimate does not include implicit orphans of abandonment (millions of children) as well as sold and/trafficked children.
- Every day 5,760 more children become orphans.
- Each year 14 million children grow up as orphans and age out of the system by age sixteen. They have no family to belong to, and no place to call home.
- 10% to 15% of aged-out orphans committed suicide before they reach age eighteen; 60% of the girls become prostitutes, and 70% of the boys become hardened criminals.

USA Data [12 & 13]

- Over 25 million American children are being raised in a family without a father

- 50% of youth in shelters and on the streets reported that their parents either told them to leave or know they were leaving but did not care.
- As many as 2.8 million children live on the streets, a third of whom are lured into prostitution within eight hours of leaving home.
- One in eight youth under the age of eighteen will leave home and become homeless in need of service.

Islamic Stance on the Treatment of Orphans

Orphans in the Quran

Taking care of orphans is an act of piety in Islamic thought. The Quran emphasizes repeatedly (23 times in 12 Surah) the importance of taking care of orphans as shown in the following examples:

- Spending on the orphans is included in a high priority list and it is a clear indication of piety:

يَسْـَٔلُونَكَ مَاذَا يُنفِقُونَ قُلْ مَآ أَنفَقْتُم مِّنْ خَيْرٍ فَلِلْوَ لِدَيْنِ وَٱلْأَقْرَبِينَ وَٱلْيَتَـٰمَىٰ وَٱلْمَسَـٰكِينِ وَٱبْنِ ٱلسَّبِيلِ وَمَا تَفْعَلُواْ مِنْ خَيْرٍ فَإِنَّ ٱللَّهَ بِهِۦ عَلِيمٌ

"They ask you (Prophet) what they should spend on others. Say: 'Whatever of your wealth you spend should be for parents, close relatives, orphans, the needy, and the wayfarer; God is well aware of whatever good you do.'"
(2:215)

لَّيْسَ ٱلْبِرَّ أَن تُوَلُّواْ وُجُوهَكُمْ قِبَلَ ٱلْمَشْرِقِ وَٱلْمَغْرِبِ وَلَـٰكِنَّ ٱلْبِرَّ مَنْ ءَامَنَ بِٱللَّهِ وَٱلْيَوْمِ ٱلْءَاخِرِ وَٱلْمَلَـٰٓئِكَةِ وَٱلْكِتَـٰبِ وَٱلنَّبِيِّۦنَ وَءَاتَى ٱلْمَالَ عَلَىٰ حُبِّهِۦ ذَوِى ٱلْقُرْبَىٰ وَٱلْيَتَـٰمَىٰ وَٱلْمَسَـٰكِينَ وَٱبْنَ ٱلسَّبِيلِ وَٱلسَّآئِلِينَ وَفِى ٱلرِّقَابِ

"True piety does not consist in turning your faces toward the east or the west in prayers-but the truly pious are those who believe in God, the Last Day, the Angels, the Scripture, and the Prophets; who give away some of their wealth, however much they cherish it, to their

4

relatives, to the orphans, the needy, the wayfarers, the beggars, and to liberate those in bondage." (2:177)

- Supporting orphans is among the traits of the true believers:

وَيُطْعِمُونَ ٱلطَّعَامَ عَلَىٰ حُبِّهِ مِسْكِينًا وَيَتِيمًا وَأَسِيرًا ﴿٨﴾ إِنَّمَا نُطْعِمُكُمْ لِوَجْهِ ٱللَّهِ لَا نُرِيدُ مِنكُمْ جَزَآءً وَلَا شُكُورًا ﴿٩﴾ إِنَّا نَخَافُ مِن رَّبِّنَا يَوْمًا عَبُوسًا قَمْطَرِيرًا ﴿١٠﴾

"They give food to the poor, the orphan, and the captive, despite their love to it (the food), saying: 'We feed you for the sake of God alone. We seek neither recompense nor thanks from you. We fear the Day of our Lord - a distressful, woefully grim Day'" (76:8-10)

- Treat orphans with kindness and be conscious to God when dealing with them:

فَأَمَّا ٱلْيَتِيمَ فَلَا تَقْهَرْ

"So do not be harsh with the orphan." (93:9).

وَلْيَخْشَ ٱلَّذِينَ لَوْ تَرَكُوا مِنْ خَلْفِهِمْ ذُرِّيَّةً ضِعَٰفًا خَافُوا عَلَيْهِمْ فَلْيَتَّقُوا ٱللَّهَ وَلْيَقُولُوا قَوْلًا سَدِيدًا

"Let those guardians who would fear for the future of their own helpless children, if they were to die, show the same concern for orphans; let them be conscious of God and speak out for justice." (4:9).

Orphans in the Sunnah

There are numerous *Hadiths* of the Prophet (*pbuh*) urging good treatment of orphans, as shown in the following examples [7]:

- The Prophet (*pbuh*) said: "the best of Muslims' homes is the one in which an orphan is well treated; and the worst one is that in which he is maltreated". (*Ibn Majah and Al Bukhary*)

- The Prophet (*pbuh*) said: "One who pats an orphan's head for God's sake will be credited with good deeds equal to the hair of the orphan. One who treats an orphan boy or a girl well he and I will be together in Paradise like this" and he joined his two fingers as illustration (*Ahmad and Tirmidhi*)

- The Prophet (*pbuh*) said: "one who shares his food and drink with an orphan is bound to enter Paradise, unless he committed an unforgivable sin."

- A man confessed to the Prophet (*pbuh*) about his hard-heartiness. The Prophet directed him to pat on an orphan's head, and to feed the poor (*Ahmad*)

Islamic Legal Rulings to Support Orphans

The Quran gives specific rules about the legal relationship between a child and his or her caring family, as described in the following verses:

مَّا جَعَلَ ٱللَّهُ لِرَجُلٍ مِّن قَلْبَيْنِ فِي جَوْفِهِۦ وَمَا جَعَلَ أَزْوَٰجَكُمُ ٱلَّٰٓـِٔى تُظَٰهِرُونَ مِنْهُنَّ أُمَّهَٰتِكُمْ وَمَا جَعَلَ أَدْعِيَآءَكُمْ أَبْنَآءَكُمْ ذَٰلِكُمْ قَوْلُكُم بِأَفْوَٰهِكُمْ وَٱللَّهُ يَقُولُ ٱلْحَقَّ وَهُوَ يَهْدِي ٱلسَّبِيلَ ﴿٤﴾ ٱدْعُوهُمْ لِءَابَآئِهِمْ هُوَ أَقْسَطُ عِندَ ٱللَّهِ فَإِن لَّمْ تَعْلَمُوٓا۟ ءَابَآءَهُمْ فَإِخْوَٰنُكُمْ فِى ٱلدِّينِ وَمَوَٰلِيكُمْ وَلَيْسَ عَلَيْكُمْ جُنَاحٌ فِيمَآ أَخْطَأْتُم بِهِۦ وَلَٰكِن مَّا تَعَمَّدَتْ قُلُوبُكُمْ وَكَانَ ٱللَّهُ غَفُورًا رَّحِيمًا ﴿٥﴾

"God did not make any man with two hearts in his body, nor did He make your wives whom you make estranged to be as your mothers, nor did He make your adopted children to be your sons. These are only words from your mouths, but God speaks the truth, and He guides people to the right path. Name your adopted sons after their (biological) fathers - that is more just with God. But if you do not

know their fathers, then, name them as your brothers in faith and your patrons. You will not be blamed if you make a mistake in this respect, but you will be responsible only for what your hearts deliberately intend- for God indeed is most forgiving and merciful."
(33: 4 - 5)

The above Quranic verses imply the following rules [14-15]:

- An orphan child retains his or her own biological family name and does not change it to match that of the caring family.
- An orphan child inherits from his or her biological parents, but not from the caring parents.
- The blood relationship rules of modesty and marriage restrictions applied to biological family members (Cf. the 4th Quranic Commandment in volume I) are not applied to grown up orphans in caring homes.
- A guardian should make it clear that his relationship with the orphan in his or her charge is a guardianship one, and he or she should not create the impression that the orphans are their real children- thus, maintaining their true identity.
- Making a mistake in the orphan's identity, or by calling him or her out of love "my son" or "my daughter" is forgivable as long as the guardian's intention is clear and sincere.

Based on the above rules, legal adoption is not permitted in Islam. Instead, *Shari'ah* permits a system of guardianship, called *"kafalah"*, which resembles foster-parenting. In Arabic, the word *"kafalah"* has two distinct meanings: to guarantee (*dhaman*) and to take care of (*rea'yah*). The person who carries on the obligations of the *kafalah* is called *"kafeel"*.

Kafalah is defined as the voluntary commitment to take care of the maintenance, the education, and the protection of a child (male or female), in the same way as a father would do for his own biological child [16]. Thus, *kafalah* involves the obligations of guardianship and maintenance without the creation of legal ties that would produce specific personal legal entitlements; in particular, the child name and his or her inheritance. Unlike foster-parenting, *kafalah* is intended to be a permanent arrangement for the minor. Like foster-parenting, *kafalah* could be facilitated by the state.

Kafalah can also be committed to an orphan without he or she is joining a *kafeel's* family. This can be done through donations to the institutions charged with caring for orphans.

In Islam, an orphan's *kafalah* is considered a highly regarded good deed, particularly if the orphan shares the life with the *kafeel* and his or her family. According to a Prophet's *Hadith*, heavenly rewards await those who take care of orphans. The Prophet (*pbuh*) is said to have noted: "The *kafeel* of an orphan and I will be together in heaven like this" and he placed his middle and index fingers side by side (*Al-Bukhary*).

The Orphan's Wealth
(*Mal al-Yateem*)

Definition

The Arabic word "*mal*" is translated in English to 'wealth' that means all property own by a person that have a money value or an exchangeable value [7&8].

Sources of the Orphan's Wealth

The *Shari'ah* has defined the following sources of orphan's wealth:

1. Their own inheritance (*al-meerath*) based on the rules revealed in Surah *An-nisa*:

لِّلرِّجَالِ نَصِيبٌ مِّمَّا تَرَكَ ٱلْوَ لِدَانِ وَٱلْأَقْرَبُونَ وَلِلنِّسَآءِ نَصِيبٌ مِّمَّا تَرَكَ ٱلْوَ لِدَانِ وَٱلْأَقْرَبُونَ مِمَّا قَلَّ مِنْهُ أَوْ كَثُرَ ۚ نَصِيبًا مَّفْرُوضًا

"Men shall have a share in what their parents and closed relatives leave, and women shall have a share in what their parents and closed relatives leave, whether the legacy be small or large- (this is) a share ordained (by God)." (4:7)

2. Voluntary provisions from the inheritance of others:

وَإِذَا حَضَرَ ٱلْقِسْمَةَ أُوْلُواْ ٱلْقُرْبَىٰ وَٱلْيَتَٰمَىٰ وَٱلْمَسَٰكِينُ فَٱرْزُقُوهُم مِّنْهُ
وَقُولُواْ لَهُمْ قَوْلًا مَّعْرُوفًا

*"And if the distribution is attended by the relatives, the
orphans, and the needy, then you shall give them part of it,
and speak to them kindly"* (4:8).

3. Provision of voluntary charities (*sadaqat*) offered by wealthy or
   financially capable individuals to sponsor orphans as stated in the
   Quranic verses (2:215) & (2:177).

4. Islamic state provisions dedicated to social improvement
   programs for the orphans and the needy:

مَّآ أَفَآءَ ٱللَّهُ عَلَىٰ رَسُولِهِۦ مِنْ أَهْلِ ٱلْقُرَىٰ فَلِلَّهِ وَلِلرَّسُولِ وَلِذِى ٱلْقُرْبَىٰ
وَٱلْيَتَٰمَىٰ وَٱلْمَسَٰكِينِ وَٱبْنِ ٱلسَّبِيلِ كَىْ لَا يَكُونَ دُولَةًۢ بَيْنَ ٱلْأَغْنِيَآءِ مِنكُمْ

*"And whatever gains God provided to His messenger from
the people of the townships (spoils taken), it shall be turned
over to God and His Messenger, and the relatives (of
deceased believers), and the orphans, and the needy, and the
traveler in need. Thus, it will not remain monopolized by the
rich among you."* (59: 7).

Management of the Orphan's Wealth

When an orphan has inherited some wealth, his or her guardian (*al-
Walei*) is responsible for protecting it until he or she reaches an age
of maturity and full mental and physical strengths. The guardian is a
family member, such as the grandfather, delegated by the *Shari'ah* to
take care of the orphan, and to act on his or her behalf in financial
matters. For an abandoned child, the state (the government of the
Muslim community) is acting as his or her guardian.

In some cases, the guardian may appoint a custodian (*Wasi*) to control
and manage the financial affairs of the orphan. However, the orphan,
not the guardian, has legal title to the property.

Guidelines to Approach the Orphan's Wealth

General Rules

God (*SWT*) says:

وَيَسْـَٔلُونَكَ عَنِ ٱلْيَتَـٰمَىٰ ۖ قُلْ إِصْلَاحٌ لَّهُمْ خَيْرٌ ۖ وَإِن تُخَالِطُوهُمْ فَإِخْوَٰنُكُمْ ۚ وَٱللَّهُ يَعْلَمُ ٱلْمُفْسِدَ مِنَ ٱلْمُصْلِحِ ۚ وَلَوْ شَآءَ ٱللَّهُ لَأَعْنَتَكُمْ ۚ إِنَّ ٱللَّهَ عَزِيزٌ حَكِيمٌ

"And they ask you regarding the orphans. Say: 'It is good to set things right for them, and if you are to care for them, then they are your brothers.' God knows those who corrupt things and those who improve them. And had God so willed, He could have imposed hardships that you would not be able to bear. God is Noble and Wise." (2:220).

The implications of this verse are the following [17]:

- The guardian should always look for improving the conditions of the orphan in his charge and do whatever is best for his or her interest.
- If a guardian shares the wealth of an orphan in his charge, he is permitted to benefit by such association, e.g. through a business partnership, provided this does not harm the orphan's interests in any way.
- Being members of the larger family of Islam, orphans should always be treated in a spirit of fraternity and brotherhood.
- God (*SWT*) is the judge of people's motives and intentions. He does recognize those who are genuine and who are not; so guardians should always be conscious of God in dealing with the orphan's affairs.

Consuming (*Ak'l*) the Orphan's Wealth by the Guardian

God (*SWT*) says:

وَمَن كَانَ غَنِيًّا فَلْيَسْتَعْفِفْ ۖ وَمَن كَانَ فَقِيرًا فَلْيَأْكُلْ بِٱلْمَعْرُوفِ

"if the guardian is rich he should abstain from consuming the orphan's property, and if he is poor, he should take only what is fair" (4:6)

God (*SWT*) says:

إِنَّ ٱلَّذِينَ يَأْكُلُونَ أَمْوَٰلَ ٱلْيَتَـٰمَىٰ ظُلْمًا إِنَّمَا يَأْكُلُونَ فِى بُطُونِهِمْ نَارًا ۖ وَسَيَصْلَوْنَ سَعِيرًا

"Those who consume the property of orphans unjustly are actually swallowing fire into their own bellies; they will endure the blazing Flame." (4:10)

The above verses indicate the following:
- A rich guardian is not allowed to touch the orphan's property as a compensation of his guardianship, and he/she should have the spiritual discipline to abstain from doing such an unjust act.
- A poor guardian is allowed to take a fair portion of the orphan's property to cover his own basic needs, or as a compensation for his guardianship efforts.
- Those people who take from the orphan's property unjustly, whether rich or poor, their ultimate destination is the blaze of Hellfire.

Mixing (*khalt*) the Orphan's Wealth with the Guardian's Wealth

God (*SWT*) says:

وَءَاتُواْ ٱلْيَتَـٰمَىٰ أَمْوَٰلَهُمْ ۖ وَلَا تَتَبَدَّلُواْ ٱلْخَبِيثَ بِٱلطَّيِّبِ ۖ وَلَا تَأْكُلُوٓاْ أَمْوَٰلَهُمْ إِلَىٰ أَمْوَٰلِكُمْ ۚ إِنَّهُ كَانَ حُوبًا كَبِيرًا

"Give the orphans their property. Do not substitute bad things of your own for their good things, and do not absorb their wealth into your own wealth. That is surely a great sin." (4:2).

11

- The guardian is ordered here to give the orphans what belong to them of property that is under his or her control. Mixing the orphan's property with the guardian's one could complicate the process of handing the property over to the orphan.
- The guardian must not absorb the wealth of the orphans, in whole or in part, by mixing it with his or her own property.
- The guardian must not exchange any good part of the orphans' property for something inferior of his or her own.
- Any of the above actions is considered to be a great sin and a criminal act which God has warned the Muslim community against.

Buying and Selling the Orphan's Property to Others

The guardian is allowed to buy and sell the orphan's property as long as he or she follows the general rules described above. In addition, Muslim jurists established the following conditions to allow the selling of the property of a minor orphan:

- The money produced from the sale of the orphan's property is needed to cover the orphan's expenses for food, clothing, education, or health care.
- The selling of the property is beneficial to the orphan's, e.g. to take advantage of a booming property market.
- The selling of the orphan's property is due to fear of its damage, theft, or neglect.
- The money is needed to fulfill the parents' promises whether written or verbally expressed. This could be in the form of paying a loan, fulfilling a will, or follow up with a commitment.

Loaning (*Iqradh*) the Orphan's Money

There is only one type of loan (*qard*) allowed in Islam that is the "*qard hasan*", an interest free (good) loan which is extended for good cause to the poor, the needy, or the distressed. It is therefore a type of a charity. Since a minor orphan is not obligated to pay a charity, his money should be invested for him/her by the guardian rather than loaning it to others.

Joint-Venture (*musharakah*) with the Orphan's Money

The guardian is allowed to invest portion of the orphan's cash money in a joint venture with another party to execute a particular business project and shares the profit gained based on a contractual agreement between the two parties. The Islamic jurists put forward the following conditions for joint-venture business deals:

- The deal is made to the best interest of the minor orphan.
- The joint venture has a specific definable objective to be achieved within a specific time period.
- The partners are reliable and the risks of failure are well understood.
- The agreement is written in legal contractual format.
- All profits gained would go to the orphan; none to the guardian.
- The guardian may take fair administrative expenses out of the orphan's profit.

Returning Wealth Over to Orphans

According to the sixth commandment, a guardian must protect and improve the orphan's property until the orphan comes of age *("attains the age of full strength"* 6:152), and becomes physically and mentally able to receive the property, and make use of it.

The stage when a person comes of age, and the conditions of handing property over to orphans, are described in the following Quranic verse:

وَٱبْتَلُواْ ٱلْيَتَـٰمَىٰ حَتَّىٰٓ إِذَا بَلَغُواْ ٱلنِّكَاحَ فَإِنْ ءَانَسْتُم مِّنْهُمْ رُشْدًا فَٱدْفَعُوٓاْ إِلَيْهِمْ أَمْوَ لَهُمْ وَلَا تَأْكُلُوهَآ إِسْرَافًا وَبِدَارًا أَن يَكْبَرُواْ وَمَن كَانَ غَنِيًّا فَلْيَسْتَعْفِفْ وَمَن كَانَ فَقِيرًا فَلْيَأْكُلْ بِٱلْمَعْرُوفِ فَإِذَا دَفَعْتُمْ إِلَيْهِمْ أَمْوَ لَهُمْ فَأَشْهِدُواْ عَلَيْهِمْ

13

وَكَفَىٰ بِٱللَّهِ حَسِيبًا

"And test the orphans when they reach a marriageable age; then, if you find them to be mature of mind, hand over to them their possessions. Do not deliberately consume them wastefully or quickly before they grow up. And if the guardian is rich, then let him not claim anything, and if he is poor, then let him consume only in goodness. When you give to them their wealth, call witnesses in; and God is enough for Reckoning." (4:6)

In this verse God (*SWT*) commands the guardian to test and examine the actions, behaviors, and attitudes of the orphan under his charge as he or she grows up and transitions from childhood to adulthood. Then, the following three conditions have been laid down for handling over the property to their owners, i.e. the orphans:

1. Attainment of Sexual Maturity – Reach Marriageable Age

Sexual maturity is the age or stage when an organism can reproduce. In human, the process of sexual maturity is termed puberty [18]. The major sign for puberty for girls is menstruation; for boys, it is the first ejaculation. On average, girls begin puberty at ages ten-eleven years; boys at ages eleven-twelve years. Girls usually complete puberty at ages fifteen-seventeen; boys at ages sixteen-seventeen.

In certain societies around the world, marriage is allowed at early signs of puberty. However, at such early ages, a child does not have the psychological, emotional, or mental capabilities to enter into marriage. In addition, marriage requires a legal contract between two consenting adults of full legal capacity. A child does not have such legal capacity. To this end, the marriage age is set at eighteen years in most countries [19]. However, most jurisdictions allow marriage at younger ages with parental and/or court approval, or in case of pregnancy.

2. Attainment of Mental and Emotional Maturity- Reach Adulthood Age

Legally, adulthood means that a person considered being mature enough to manage his or her affairs in a sound and appropriate manner to be entrusted by society with certain responsibilities. Such milestones include, but are not limited to, voting, obtaining a driver license, having serving in the military or on a jury, entering into contracts, finishing certain levels of education, purchasing or renting his own dwelling, getting married, having a job or starting a business. It is also the age at which a person is liable for his action such as contractual obligations or liability for negligence. In general, a parental or guardianship duty of a person ceases when the child reaches the age of adulthood.

In some societies, a ritual event related to the oncoming of adulthood which encompasses passing a series of tests to demonstrate that a person is mentally, emotionally and spiritually ready for adulthood [20]. Most modern societies determine legal adulthood base on reaching a specific age (normally 18 years) without requiring passing maturity tests.

3. Handing the Property Over to the Orphans in the Presence of Witnesses

Calling witnesses to attend the transfer of property from the guardian to the orphan is the third condition inducted by the above verse. Such an action would prevent false claims and future costly court disputes.

In our modern societies, Islamic courts document and register all the details of the orphans' properties under the control of the guardian and/or the custodian, review annual reports on the financial activities of the orphan's trust, and administer the legal transfer of the properties from the guardian to the mature-adult orphan. Such procedures ensure achieving the best interest of the orphans, particularly those financially inexperienced, and protect their assets from undue losses.

In addition, the Quranic verse (4:6) emphasizes the following:
- The need to hand over the orphan's property without any delay, once it has been established that an orphan is of sound judgment.
- There should be no attempt to consume the orphan's wealth by wasteful and hasty spending decisions before the orphan reaches the age of adulthood.
- There should be no administrations' fees for a rich guardian and only fair fees for a poor one.
- One should always remember that God (*SWT*) witnesses everything and He takes everything into account.

Summary

- The sixth commandment is focused on the treatment of Orphans who are the weakest elements in the society. They are boys and girls younger than 18 years old, who are left without a father or a guardian to protect their rights and provide their basic needs of food and shelter.
- Currently, there are approximately six thousand child become orphans every day, due to wars, natural disasters, poor economic conditions, and uneven distribution of wealth. As they reach the age of 18 years, 15% commit suicide, 60% of the girls become prostitutes, and 70% of the boys become hardened criminals.
- Legal adoption is not permitted in Islam, but a system of guardianship that resembles foster parenting is in place. It is called *kafalah* that is managed by a guardian (*kafeel*) who is appointed to manage the affairs of the orphan until he or she reaches the age of maturity.
- The Islamic law established guidelines for the guardian to approach the orphan's wealth, and to do whatever is best for his or her interest. When the orphan becomes physically and mentally capable of managing his or her property, then the

guardian is obliged to handle the property over to the orphan in the presence of witnesses.

References

1. Yusuf Ali, "The Holy Quran: Text, Translation and Commentary", Published in the USA by The Muslim Students Association of the United States and Canada (1975)
2. Sayyid A, Al Mawdudi, "Towards Understanding the Qur'an", translated and edited by Zafar I. Ansari, Published by the Islamic foundation, UK (1988)
3. Pickthall, "The Holy Qur-'aan" (Translation and Transliteration), Published by the Burney Academy, Hyderabad, India (1981).
4. Muhammad T. Al-Hilali & Muhammad M. Khan, "The Noble Qur'an: English Translation of the Meanings and Commentary", Published by King Fahd Complex for the printing of the Holy Qur'an, Madinah, K.S.A. (1417 H)
5. Muhammad Asad, "The Message of the Qur'an", (Translation, Transliteration, and Explanations), Published by the Book Foundation, Bristol, England (2003).
6. Sayyid Qutb, "In the Shade of the Qur'an", Translated and edited by Adil Salahi, Published by the Islamic Foundation, UK (2006).
7. Maryam A. Quzah, "Provision of the Wealth of the Orphan in Islamic Jurisprudence", Master Degree Thesis, Al-Najah National University, Nablus, Palestine (2011)- in Arabic
8. Ayman I. Sal's, "Ahkam al-Yateem fi al-Islam", Published by Dar Al-Resalah Al-A'lamiah, Damascus, Syria (2010)
9. Jamila Bargach, "Orphans of Islam", Rowman & Littlefield Publishers, Inc., Lanham, Maryland, U.S.A. (2002)
10. Muslim Women's *Shura* Council, "Adoption and the Care of Orphan Children: Islam and the Best Interest of the Child", American Soc. Of Muslim Advancements (2011).
11. Orphan Hope International, www.orphanhopeint.org/facts-statistics/
12. The Orphan Society of America (OSA) Assessment: On the State of Parentless Chidden & Youth in the U.S. (August 2007)

13. New York State Office of Children and Family Services, "Foster Parent Manual" (2010).
14. Ref. [1], notes 3671-3672, page 1163.
15. Ref. [5], notes # 4-7, page 639.
16. International Reference Center for the Rights of Children Deprived from their Family (ISS/IRC), "Specific Case: *Kafalah*", Fact Sheet No 51, (Geneva: ISS, 2007)
17. Ref. [5], notes # 206-207, page 48.
18. "Puberty", http://en.wikipedia.org/wiki/puberty.
19. "Marriageable Age", http://en.wikipedia.org/Marriageable_age.
20. "Child Marriage", http://www.forwarduk.org.uk/key-issues/child-marriage.

The Seventh Quranic Commandment
"Give full measure and weight with fairness-
We do not burden any soul with more than it can bear"

Meaning of the Words

In Arabic, the seventh Quranic commandment from Surah *Al-An'am* (6:152) reads as follows:

وَأَوْفُوا الْكَيْلَ وَالْمِيزَانَ بِالْقِسْطِ ۖ لَا نُكَلِّفُ نَفْسًا إِلَّا وُسْعَهَا

"Wa awful-kayla wal-mizana bilqist. La nukallifu nafsan illa wus'aha"

Let us examine the English translation of each Arabic word in this statement:

"wa" means "and", which implies that this 7th Commandment is in addition to the previous six Commandments; *"awfu"* is the plural grammatical format of the verb *"waf'fa"* (*n. Wafa'a*) means "fulfill", "complete" or "give full"; *"al Kayla"* is a calibrated container to measure items, particularly for dry products such as grains; *al Mizan"* is the balance used to weight items; *"bilqist"* means "with fairness"; *"La nukallifu"* means "We do not burden"; *"nafsan"* means "a soul"; *"ella"* means "except"; *"wus'aha"* means "its capability" or "what it can bear".

Accordingly, in this text, the Quranic seventh commandment is translated as follow:

> *"And give full measure and weight with fairness-*
> *We do not burden any soul with more than it can bear"*

This translation is similar to those found in Refs [1-7].

More analysis on the meaning of the words in the seventh commandment is given in the following sections.

Meaning of *"Give full measure and weight with fairness"*

This statement prohibits the manipulation of measures and weights in commercial deals. In particular, it refers to the act of giving people short measures and weights, without their knowledge. The commandment requires people and institutions to do their best to ensure that everyone gets what is fairly due to them. In our modern time, it means that the product must meet all its specifications and quality requirements to all its customers. Any changes in these specifications without the knowledge of the customers are considered fraud which is prohibited.

Since other Quranic commandments are covering different aspects of non-commercial dealings we will focus our discussions about the seventh commandment on Islamic aspects of commercial dealings, which constitute a major part of human activities.

Meaning of *"We do not burden any soul with more than it can bear"*

This statement is a well-established divine principal. It is mentioned here to emphasize the fact that anyone who tries the utmost of his ability to achieve fairness in commercial deals, in giving accurate measure and weight, will be acquitted of responsibility of unintentional mistakes or error.

Thus, people should always have the sincere intention to act rightfully, and hope for God's forgiveness for any act of forgetfulness or mistakes

لَا يُكَلِّفُ ٱللَّهُ نَفْسًا إِلَّا وُسْعَهَا ۚ لَهَا مَا كَسَبَتْ وَعَلَيْهَا مَا ٱكْتَسَبَتْ ۗ رَبَّنَا لَا تُؤَاخِذْنَآ إِن نَّسِينَآ أَوْ أَخْطَأْنَا ۚ رَبَّنَا وَلَا تَحْمِلْ عَلَيْنَآ إِصْرًا كَمَا حَمَلْتَهُۥ عَلَى ٱلَّذِينَ مِن قَبْلِنَا ۚ رَبَّنَا وَلَا تُحَمِّلْنَا مَا لَا طَاقَةَ لَنَا بِهِۦ ۖ وَٱعْفُ عَنَّا وَٱغْفِرْ لَنَا وَٱرْحَمْنَآ ۚ أَنتَ مَوْلَىٰنَا فَٱنصُرْنَا عَلَى ٱلْقَوْمِ ٱلْكَٰفِرِينَ

"God does not burden any human being with more than he is well able to bear: in his favor shall be whatever good he does, and against him whatever evil he does: 'Our Lord, do not take us to task

*if we forget or make mistakes. Our Lord, do not burden us as You
have burdened those before us. Our Lord, do not burden us with
more than we have strength to bear. Pardon us, forgive us, and have
mercy on us. You are our Protector, so grant us victory over the
disbelievers'"*. (2:286)

The Significance of the Seventh Commandment

Moral principles and code of ethics in commercial dealings are
repeatedly emphasized in the Quran. Thus, in addition to Surah *Al-
An'am* (6:152), the seventh commandment is repeated in Surah *Al-
Isra* with a slight variation as follow:

وَأَوْفُواْ ٱلْكَيْلَ إِذَا كِلْتُمْ وَزِنُواْ بِٱلْقِسْطَاسِ ٱلْمُسْتَقِيمِ ۚ ذَٰلِكَ خَيْرٌ وَأَحْسَنُ تَأْوِيلًا

*"And give full measure whenever you measure, and weigh with a
balance that is straight; that is good and better in the end."* (17:35)

The commandment is also repeated in Surah *Al-Rahman* as follow:

وَأَقِيمُوا الْوَزْنَ بِالْقِسْطِ وَلَا تُخْسِرُوا الْمِيزَانَ

"Weigh with justice and do not fall short in the balance" (55:9)

Moreover, the practice of commercial cheating is strongly condemned
in the Surah entitled *"Al-Mutaffifin"*, i.e. those who give short
measures and weights. They have been reminded with the Day of
Judgment when everyone stands before God (*SWT*):

وَيْلٌ لِّلْمُطَفِّفِينَ ﴿١﴾ الَّذِينَ إِذَا اكْتَالُوا عَلَى النَّاسِ يَسْتَوْفُونَ ﴿٢﴾ وَإِذَا كَالُوهُمْ أَو
وَّزَنُوهُمْ يُخْسِرُونَ ﴿٣﴾ أَلَا يَظُنُّ أُولَئِكَ أَنَّهُم مَّبْعُوثُونَ ﴿٤﴾ لِيَوْمٍ عَظِيمٍ ﴿٥﴾ يَوْمَ
يَقُومُ النَّاسُ لِرَبِّ الْعَالَمِينَ ﴿٦﴾

*"Woe to those who cheat. Those who when they are receiving any
measure from the people, they take it in full. And when they are the
ones giving measure or weight for others, they give less than due.*

21

Do these people not realize that they will be raised up (resurrected) on a mighty Day, a Day when everyone will stand before the Lord of the Worlds."
(83: 1-6)

In addition, the story of Prophet Shu'ayb (*pbuh*) has been repeated several times in the Quran ((7:85-87), (11:84-88), (26:176-186), and (29:36)) to remind the people about the fate of a community which incurred divine punishment for their criminal and sinful acts committed during their commercial trading deals.

Besides the Quran, there are numerous teachings of Prophet Muhammad (*pbuh*) who was an experienced trader. In addition, he established the first Islamic market in Medina and used it to observe, correct, teach, and guide the people to the right Islamic approach in commercial dealings.

Islamic Ethical Values in Commercial Dealings

In Islam, the adherence to moral codes of behavior is part of the faith (*eman*) itself. These moral codes cover literally every aspect of a Muslim life from political government to the sale of real property, from hunting to the etiquette of dining, from marriage relationships to worship and prayers. In commercial dealing, it provides a number of rules of ethical discipline without which business contracts would be regarded as lacking perfection in terms of good manners, decency and ethical excellence. Some of these moral values are briefly described below [8 & 9].

Honesty

Honesty is the quality of being sincere, transparent, and truthful. Traders need to be honest when they make deals with potential customers. They must provide full disclosure about the product or the service being offered, including both its benefits and its faults.

The Prophet (*pbuh*) was reported to have said: "The honest/truthful merchant is rewarded by being ranked on the Day of Resurrection with Prophets, pious people, and martyrs." (*Tirmidhi*).

Sellers often take recourse of swearing by God's name to emphasize the good quality of their products. Swearing in business for such purposes is prohibited in Islam, be it false or true. Thus, false swearing is an act of sin. Swearing by God (*SWT*) is too great to be used as a mean to sell merchandise. The Prophet (pbuh) was reported to have said: "Swearing may persuade the customer to purchase the goods, but the deal will be deprived of God's blessing." (*Al Bukhari*)

Trustworthiness

Trustworthiness is one of the values that is closely related to honesty and integrity of the individual. It is a moral virtue which characterizes the true believers as indicated by the following verse:

وَٱلَّذِينَ هُمْ لِأَمَـٰنَـٰتِهِمْ وَعَهْدِهِمْ رَٰعُونَ

"And those who are faithful to their trusts and to their covenants" (23:8).

Trust covers all the responsibilities which are conveyed to someone because he is trusted. These might consist of obligations arising out of an agreement or collective covenant. It might consist of a group's private data, a company's proprietary information, or a nation's military plans. It might also consist of personal or collective property, or any office or position which might be granted upon a person by a group.

In business, trust sales (*buyu' al-amanah*) are a type of sales in which the sellers under obligation to disclose to the purchasers the cost price of the product. The main purpose of trust sales is the protection of buyers and consumers who lack expertise and knowledge. Such buyer needs and agrees to buy merchandises based on trust sale from a seller who is supposed to have sufficient knowledge about the quality and the price of the goods. In return, the buyer agrees to pay a certain additional amount over and above the cost price to the seller profit. If the seller is guilty of any deception, the purchaser is entitled to cancel the contract.

Leniency

Leniency, tolerance, and forbearing are among the moral values required in conducting commercial deals. The Prophet (*pbuh*) was reported to have said: "God bestows His mercy on His servant who is lenient when he sells, lenient when he buys, and lenient when he asks for his rights (i.e. in the court)" (*Al Bukhari*).

In particular, one should be lenient with the debtor who experiences difficulty in repaying his debt. God (*SWT*) says:

وَإِن كَانَ ذُو عُسْرَةٍ فَنَظِرَةٌ إِلَىٰ مَيْسَرَةٍ ۚ وَأَن تَصَدَّقُواْ خَيْرٌ لَّكُمْ ۖ إِن كُنتُمْ تَعْلَمُونَ

"If the debtor is in difficult circumstances, then grant him a delay in payment until a time of ease; still if you were to write it off as an act of charity; that would be better for you, if only you knew." (2:280)

In turn, the debtor should also give back the debt to the creditor on time with due thanks and politeness. The Prophet (*pbuh*) was the best of all people in repaying the debts as shown by the following event reported by *Abou Hurayrah*:

"The Prophet (*pbuh*) took a young camel on a loan from a man. This man came to the Prophet asking him harshly to return his camel. The man's disrespectful approach angered the Prophet's companions and they stood up to punish him. The Prophet said: 'let him go; it is his right to speak'. Then, he asked his companions to give the creditor a she camel younger than his. They pointed out that there were no young camels left except for a four-year old one of a very good quality. The Prophet (*pbuh*) said: 'Give him the best one, for the best amongst you is who repays the rights of other handsomely.'" (*Muslim*)

24

Based on this *Hadith*, Muslim Jurists legalized and even encouraged repayment of a loan with an extra amount over and above its value, as long as this addition was not stated as a condition for the loan.

Justice

God (*SWT*) says:

إِنَّ ٱللَّهَ يَأْمُرُ بِٱلْعَدْلِ وَٱلْإِحْسَـٰنِ
"God commands justice and goodness" (16:90)

God (*SWT*) commands justice at all times, to all people, Muslim and non-Muslims, and for all kinds of dealings, commercials and non-commercials.

According to the Quran and the Sunnah, a completely just society was established during the time of the Prophet (*pbuh*) and his companions. Every member of the society was treated equally; no difference existed between poor and rich, Muslim and non-Muslim, ruler and citizens. All forms of discrimination were considered unjust and strongly denounced. Prophet Muhammad (*pbuh*) declared that "No Arab has superiority over any non-Arab, and no non-Arab has superiority over an Arab; no black person has superiority over a white person, and no white person has superiority over a black person. The criterion for honor in the sight of God is righteousness and honest living".

Islamic commercial ethics strive to promote a society in which all stakeholders were treated justly. Examples are sharing profit and loss between financial institutions and its customers, the sharing of risk among all participants in a *takaful* (Islamic insurance) fund, and preventing unjust by prohibiting usury, price fixing, and hoarding.

Remembrance of God

Among the Islamic values that should not be ignored by the traders is the continuous remembrance of God (*SWT*). Thus, closing business deals and making millions in profits should not be reasons for forgetting our obligations towards God for worship and obedience. In particular, obligatory prayers should be made on time to maintain the connection with Him at all times. To this end, God (*SWT*) blesses the believers who carry on their prayers at the houses of worship where His name is constantly glorified:

فِى بُيُوتٍ أَذِنَ ٱللَّهُ أَن تُرْفَعَ وَيُذْكَرَ فِيهَا ٱسْمُهُۥ يُسَبِّحُ لَهُۥ فِيهَا بِٱلْغُدُوِّ وَٱلْءَاصَالِ

رِجَالٌ لَّا تُلْهِيهِمْ تِجَٰرَةٌ وَلَا بَيْعٌ عَن ذِكْرِ ٱللَّهِ وَإِقَامِ ٱلصَّلَوٰةِ وَإِيتَآءِ ٱلزَّكَوٰةِ

يَخَافُونَ يَوْمًا تَتَقَلَّبُ فِيهِ ٱلْقُلُوبُ وَٱلْأَبْصَٰرُ

لِيَجْزِيَهُمُ ٱللَّهُ أَحْسَنَ مَا عَمِلُوا۟ وَيَزِيدَهُم مِّن فَضْلِهِۦ

وَٱللَّهُ يَرْزُقُ مَن يَشَآءُ بِغَيْرِ حِسَابٍ

"In houses that God has allowed to be erected, and His name mentioned in them. He is glorified therein day and night. Men who are not distracted either by trade or sale from the remembrance of God, keeping up the prayers, and paying alms (Zakah), they fear a day when the hearts and sight will be overturned. God will reward such people according to the best of their deeds, and He will give them more of His bounty; God provides limitlessly for anyone He wills." (24:36-38)

And God (*SWT*) said regarding the Friday congregation prayer:

يَٰٓأَيُّهَا ٱلَّذِينَ ءَامَنُوٓا۟ إِذَا نُودِىَ لِلصَّلَوٰةِ مِن يَوْمِ ٱلْجُمُعَةِ فَٱسْعَوْا۟ إِلَىٰ ذِكْرِ ٱللَّهِ

وَذَرُوا۟ ٱلْبَيْعَ ذَٰلِكُمْ خَيْرٌ لَّكُمْ إِن كُنتُمْ تَعْلَمُونَ

فَإِذَا قُضِيَتِ ٱلصَّلَوٰةُ فَٱنتَشِرُوا۟ فِى ٱلْأَرْضِ وَٱبْتَغُوا۟ مِن فَضْلِ ٱللَّهِ وَٱذْكُرُوا۟ ٱللَّهَ

كَثِيرًا لَّعَلَّكُمْ تُفْلِحُونَ

وَإِذَا رَأَوْا۟ تِجَٰرَةً أَوْ لَهْوًا ٱنفَضُّوٓا۟ إِلَيْهَا وَتَرَكُوكَ قَآئِمًا قُلْ مَا عِندَ ٱللَّهِ خَيْرٌ مِّنَ

ٱللَّهْوِ وَمِنَ ٱلتِّجَٰرَةِ وَٱللَّهُ خَيْرُ ٱلرَّٰزِقِينَ

"You who believe: When the call to prayer is made on Friday (the day of congregation), hurry towards the remembrance of God and leave off your trading-that is for your own good, if only you knew-and when the prayer has ended, disperse in the land and seek out God's bounty. Remember God often so that you may prosper. Yet they scatter towards trade or entertainment whenever they observe

it, and leave you (Prophet) standing there. Say: 'That which is with God is better than any entertainment or trade; God is the best of providers.'" (62: 9-11)

Except during the time of Friday prayer, Muslims are allowed to work for their worldly life and struggle to get wealth through buying and selling for all days of the week including Fridays. But they are commanded to stop their worldly affairs and hurry to the mosque as soon as they hear the final call (this is the call that is followed by the Imam's sermon) of Friday congregation prayer. When the prayer is completed, they can return back to their business or trade activities.

Principles of Business Conduct in Islamic Financial Institutions

Islam allows for a free-market economy where supply and demands are decided in the market- not dictated by the government. But at the same time, Islam directs the function of the market by imposing specific laws and ethics to promote social justice in the society.

In this section, seven basic principles will be presented that Islamic financial institutions must follow to distinguish themselves from conventional (secular) financial firms. For more detailed discussion on the subject of the Islamic economic system, the reader may refer to books written by Abdul-Rahman [10], Saleem [11], Al-Qaradawi [8 &12], Jamaldeen [13], and Kamali [14].

1. Prohibition of Usury (*Riba*)

Usury is defined as the lending of money with an interest charge for its use. In Islam any trade or transaction agreement based on interest is prohibited.

God (*SWT*) has warned that those who practice usury are at war with God and His Apostle:

يَـٰٓأَيُّهَا ٱلَّذِينَ ءَامَنُوا۟ ٱتَّقُوا۟ ٱللَّهَ وَذَرُوا۟ مَا بَقِىَ مِنَ ٱلرِّبَوٰٓا۟ إِن كُنتُم مُّؤْمِنِينَ
فَإِن لَّمْ تَفْعَلُوا۟ فَأْذَنُوا۟ بِحَرْبٍ مِّنَ ٱللَّهِ وَرَسُولِهِۦ ۖ وَإِن تُبْتُمْ فَلَكُمْ رُءُوسُ أَمْوَٰلِكُمْ
لَا تَظْلِمُونَ وَلَا تُظْلَمُونَ

27

"O' you who believe: be conscious of God and give up any outstanding dues from usury, if you are true believers. If you do not, then be warned of a war from God and His Messenger. If you repent, you shall have your capital without suffering loss or causing others to suffer loss." (2:278-279)

يَٰٓأَيُّهَا ٱلَّذِينَ ءَامَنُوا۟ لَا تَأْكُلُوا۟ ٱلرِّبَوٰٓا۟ أَضْعَٰفًا مُّضَٰعَفَةً ۖ وَٱتَّقُوا۟ ٱللَّهَ لَعَلَّكُمْ تُفْلِحُونَ

"You who believe: 'Do not consume usurious interest, doubled and redoubled. Be mindful of God so that you may prosper" (3:130)

Also, according to the Sunnah, the offence of charging, taking, paying, or even acting as a scribe or a witness in an interest-based (*riba*) transactions is considered one of the worst offences in the Islamic faith.

Usury is prohibited because it creates injustice in the society through oppression and exploitation of the needy. In effect, the payment of interest makes the rich becomes richer and the poor is left behind. In addition, lending money is not in itself a productive economic activity. Instead, Islamic laws recommend profit–and-loss sharing contract.

2. Prohibition of Price Fixing

Price fixing, also called price manipulation (*al talaub bil asa'r*), is a conspiracy among competitors (sellers) through the following tactics:
  a) sell a good, a service, or a commodity at the same price
  b) use the same formulas for computing selling prices
  c) offer the same discounts
  d) keep the same price differentials between different order quantities, or types
  e) notify other conspirators before making any changes in the price.

The purpose of price fixing is to coordinate pricing for mutual benefit of the traders by controlling the supply and demand in the market.

In Islam, the market is permitted to respond to the natural laws of supply and demand. It is reported that once in the Prophet's time the prices shot up high, and the people asked the Prophet to fix the prices for them. He replied: "Allah is the One Who fixes prices, Who withholds, Who gives lavishly, and Who provides, and I hope that when I meet Him none of you will have a claim against me for any injustice with regard to blood or property." (*Tirmidhi*)

The above *Hadith* does not mean that price control is prohibited regardless of the circumstances, even if it removes harm and prevents obvious injustice. Thus, in certain cases, price control may be permissible in order to meet the need of the society and to protect it from greedy opportunists.

3. Prohibition of Hoarding (*Ihtikar*)

In economics, hoarding is the practice of obtaining and holding scarce resources, so that they can be sold to customers for excessive profit. For example, a few traders operating in the market buy the entire quantity of an item, e.g. rice, and store it with the intent of selling it later at the time of scarcity to draw maximum profit.

Another form of hoarding is when a trader gets an exclusive agreement with a supplier to be the only seller to his products. He is therefore in a position to dictate his terms in the market, and sell them at an extremely high price to the needy people.

Islam strongly condemned hoarding and the Prophet (*pbuh*) is reported to denounce its practice in very strong words, as shown in the following two examples:

    a. The Prophet (*pbuh*) said: "If anyone withholds goods until the price rises, he is a sinner." (*Abou Da'wood*). It should be noted that the term "sinner" has been applied in the Quran to describe some of the vicious tyrants in the history of mankind, such as Pharaoh and Haman in Surah *Al Qasas* (the Story) (28:8).

b. The Prophet (*pbuh*) said: "He who brings goods to the market is blessed with bounty, but he who withholds them is cursed" (*Ibn Majah*)

4. Prohibition of Deceptive Transactions (*Al Gharar*)

Gharar literally means "uncertainty", "ambiguity", "danger" or "peril". Thus, a *gharar* sale is defined as "the sale of reliable items whose existence or characteristics are not certain, the risky nature of which makes the transaction similar to gambling.

Gharar is prohibited because these types of transactions are ambiguous; one or both parties do not have complete knowledge about the product or about what to expect. Had the information been fully disclosed, the buyer might not have purchased them. These transactions may give rise to disputes and disagreements between the concerned parties.

To avoid the possibility of *gharar*, Muslim jurists have laid down various conditions for different contracts. For example, the quantity and quality of the product, its basic ingredients, its price, its production, its expiration dates, and any other related and necessary details that must be clearly defined, displayed, and shared.

5. Prohibition of Gambling Transactions

The Arabic equivalent to gambling is "*Maysir*" which literarily means getting something too easily without any effort. Dice, lottery, prize bonds, betting on horse races and sport matches are to be held within the definition of gambling.

In gambling, the winner and the loser win or lose by mere chance and there is no exchange of counter-values between them. This gives rise to hostility, hatred and enmity between the winners and the losers. Consequently, Islam prohibits all gambling or gamble-like transactions and encourages people to earn their living through work and honest efforts. The Prophet (pbuh) was reported to have said: "The best earning is where a person earns through his own hands (work)".

6. Prohibition of Bribery (*Rashwa*)

In a free-market, one should not try to seek illegitimate advantages or benefits by bribing the authorities. It is a form of corruption which is strongly condemned. God (*SWT*) says:

$$وَلَا تَأْكُلُوا أَمْوَالَكُم بَيْنَكُم بِالْبَاطِلِ وَتُدْلُوا بِهَا إِلَى الْحُكَّامِ لِتَأْكُلُوا فَرِيقًا مِّنْ أَمْوَالِ النَّاسِ بِالْإِثْمِ وَأَنتُمْ تَعْلَمُونَ$$

"And do not consume your property unjustly nor give bribery to the authorities so that you may sinfully and knowingly consume a part of the property of others." (2:188)

Also, the Prophet (*pbuh*) was reported to have said: "Allah's curse is on those who give and those who take bribes".

7. Prohibition of Unlawful (*Haram*) Items

Muslims are forbidden to own, use, consume, produce manufacturing, import, or export unlawful (*haram*) items or any products that contain unlawful (*haram)* elements. Examples are the following:

- Swine, liquors and intoxicants and other prohibited foods and drinks in general.
- The meat of any bird or animal dead from natural causes, without being slaughtered in an Islamic way.
- Spoiled, contaminated, and expired foods and drinks
- Items identified by medical specialists as harmful to human health and may result in serious deceases

- Prohibited media materials (magazines, movies, videos, books, etc.) which advocate for the spreading of shameful deeds in the society.
- Boycotted items supplied by the enemies who are in active war with the Muslim community.
- Items that are known to be stolen or taken unjustly from its owner.

Prohibited Pre-Islamic Sales and Practices

The following are examples of pre-Islamic sale practices that were prohibited by the Prophet (*pbuh*) [15 & 16] because they were inconsistence with the Islamic moral values emphasized by the seventh commandment:

Covering up Defected Items

The Prophet (*pbuh*) passed by a pile of food in the market. He put his hand inside the pile and he felt dampness, although the surface of the pile was dry. He said: "Owner of the food! What is this? The man said: 'O Messenger of Allah, it was damaged by rain.' The Prophet said: 'Why did you not put the rain-damaged food on top so that people could see it?! Whoever cheats is not one of us" (*Saheeh Muslim*)

The Practice of Trickery (*Al-Najash*)

In an auction sale, a person offers a high price for something that he does not have the intention to buy it, but just to trick another person. This trickery is prohibited based on the Prophet (*pbuh*) saying: "Do not harbor envy against one another; do not outbid one another (with the goal of raising the price); do not bear enmity against one another; do not bear enmity against one another; one of you should not enter into a transaction when the other has already enter into it; and be fellow brothers and true servants of Allah" (*Muslim*)

The Exploitation of One's Ignorance of Market Conditions

As an example of this case is a newcomer to the town who is persuaded by a local trader to transfer all of his merchandise to him so that he will sell them on his behalf in the market. The trader gets the commodities on a price that is much lower than the market price, and then sells them at an exorbitant price. The Prophet (*pbuh*) said: "A town dweller should not sell the goods of a desert dweller" (*Al Bukhari*).

Sale by Force (*Bai' al-Mudtar*)

It is to buy an item forcibly or to purchase a thing when its owner is compelled under stress of want to dispose it off. Instead of purchasing the item, and taking undue advantage of the seller's helplessness, one should help him.

The Prophet (*pbuh*) said: "A Muslim should not make sales deals against each other" (*Al-Bukhari and Muslim*). This *Hadith* implies that when one person has sold goods to another, a third person should not upset the bargain trying to sell his own goods to the latter, offering them at lower rates or pointing out the defect in the goods already sold to him by the former.

Summary

- The seventh Quranic commandment is focused on the ethics of commercial deals that is covering property, merchandise or services. The commandment prohibits the manipulation of measures and weights and demands people and institutions to do their best to ensure that everyone gets what is fairly due to them.
- Commercial dealings in Islam are based on a number of basic rules of ethical discipline that are essential to carry on business deals with good manner, decency and ethical excellence. These values include honesty, trustworthiness, leniency, justice, and the continuous remembrance of God (*SWT*).

- To achieve social justice in the society in a free-market economy, Islamic law prohibited usury (*reba*), price fixing, hoarding (*ihtikar*), deceptive transactions (*al gharar*), gambling transactions, bribery, and dealing with unlawful (*haram*) items.
- The Islamic law led down specific guidelines for each element of a sale transaction, i.e. the seller, the buyer, the subject matter of the sale, its contract validation and /or its termination.
- The Prophet (*pbuh*) prohibited a number of pre-Islamic sale practices that were inconsistence with the moral values of the seventh commandment.

References

1. Yusuf Ali, "The Holy Quran: Text, Translation and Commentary", Published in the USA by The Muslim Students Association of the United States and Canada (1975)
2. Sayyid A. Al Mawdudi, "Towards Understanding the Qur'an", translated and edited by Zafar I. Ansari, Published by the Islamic foundation, UK (1988)
3. Pickthall, "The Holy Qur-'aan" (Translation and Transliteration), Published by the Burney Academy, Hyderabad, India (1981).
4. Muhammad T. Al-Hilali and Muhammad M. Khan, "The Noble Qur'an: English Translation of the Meanings and Commentary", Published by King Fahd Complex for the printing of the Holy Qur'an, Medina, K.S.A. (1417 H) .
5. Muhammad Asad, "The Message of the Qur'an", (Translation, Transliteration, and Explanations), Published by the Book Foundation, Bristol, England (2003).
6. Sayed Qutb, "In the Shade of the Qur'an", Translated and edited by Adil Salahi, Published by the Islamic Foundation, UK (2006).
7. M.A.S. Abdel Haleem, "The Quran: English Translation and Parallel Arabic Text", Published by Oxford University Press, New York, N.Y. (2010).
8. Yusuf Al Qaradawi, "*Daur al qe'yam wa al akhlaq fi al eqtisad al Islami*" (The Role of Values and Morals in the

Islamic Economy), Published in Arabic by Al Resalah Published House, Beirut, Lebanon (1999)

9. Sabahuddin Azmi, "An Islamic Approach to Business Ethics",
www.renaissance.com.pk/Mayviewpoint2y5.htm

10. Y. Abdul-Rahman, "The Art of Islamic Banking and Finance", Published by John Wiley and Sons, Inc., www.wiley.com (2010)

11. Muhammad Yusuf Saleem, "Islamic Commercial Laws", Published by John Wiley and Sons, Inc, www.wiley.com (2013)

12. Yusuf Al-Qaradawi, "The Lawful and the Prohibited in Islam", American Trust Publications, Plainfield, Indiana, USA (1994)

13. Faleel Jamaldeen, "Islamic Finance for Dummies", Published by John Wiley and Sons, Inc. www.wiley.com (2012)

14. Hashim Kamali, "Islamic Commercial Law: An Analysis of Futures and Options", Published by Islamic Text Society, Cambridge CB22 5EN, UK (2000)

15. Abou Bakr J. Al-Jaza'iry, "Minhaj Al-Muslim", Published in English by Darusslam, Riyadh, Saudi Arabia, (2001) Vol.2, pp 199-213.

16. "Translation of Sahih Muslim"-Book 10: The Book of Transactions (*Kitab Al-Buyu*), Center of Muslim-Jewish Engagement www.usc.edu/org/cmje/religious-texts/hadith/muslim/010-s...

The Eighth Quranic Commandment
"Speak justly; even if it concerns a close relative"

Meaning of the Words

In Arabic the eighth Quranic commandment from Surah *Al-An'am* (6:152) reads as follows:

وَإِذَا قُلْتُمْ فَاعْدِلُوا وَلَوْ كَانَ ذَا قُرْبَىٰ

"Wa idha qultum fa'adilu wa la'w kana dha qurba."

Let us examine the English translation of each Arabic word in this statement:

"*wa*" means "and", which implies that this 8th Commandment is in addition to the previous seven commandments; "*idha*" means "if"; "*qultum*" is the plural grammatical format of the verb "*yaqoula*" which would be translated as "if you <u>say</u> something", "if you <u>tell</u> someone", or "to <u>speak</u> in a serious and formal situation"; "*fa'adilu*" means "be just" or "be fair"; "*wa la'w*" means "even though"; "*kana*" means "*it be*"; and "*dha qurba*" means "a close relative".

Accordingly, the Quranic eighth commandment would be translated as follows:

"And whenever you speak, speak justly, even if it concerns a close relative"

The statement combines all human dealings and communications through speech. These include a person's speech as a judge, as a witness, as a mediator, as a reporter, as a critic, as a consultant, as an examiner, as a recorder, or for just voicing an opinion in any subject.

Other English translations of the eighth commandment include the followings: *"And whenever ye speak, speak fairly, even if a near relative is concerned"* [1]; *"When you speak, be just, even though it concerns a near of kin"* [2]; *"And if ye give your word, do justice thereunto, even though it be (against) a kinsman"* [3]; *"And whenever you give your word (i.e. judge between men, or give evidence), say the truth even if a near relative is concerned"*[4]; *"When you speak, be just, even though it be against one of your close relatives"* [5]; *"And when you voice an opinion, be just, even though it be (against) one of near kin"* [6]; and *"When you speak, be just, even if it concerns a relative"* [7].

Let us examine the statement of the Eighth commandment in more details.

Meaning of "and whenever you speak" (*wa idha qultum*)

In this text, the use of the conjunction "if" (*idha*) implies that one has the choice to stay silent, especially when his speech would serve no purpose [8]. Thus, the Prophet (*pbuh*) emphasized the relative value of silence in numerous *hadiths* on this subject, including the following:

- "Whoever believes in God and the Last Day should speak a good word or remain silent." (*Sahih Muslim*)

- "Part of the quality of a person's Islam is to remain silent about that which does not concern him." (*Tirmidhi*)

Thus, believers are encouraged to speak out, but only if this serves a worthy purpose. Indeed, the Quran provides guidance for testimony in courts or expressing an opinion as follow:

- If you speak, **be conscious to God,** relevant, and to the point:

يَـٰٓأَيُّهَا ٱلَّذِينَ ءَامَنُوا۟ ٱتَّقُوا۟ ٱللَّهَ وَقُولُوا۟ قَوْلًا سَدِيدًا

*"O' you who believe: Remain conscious of God, and always speak
in a direct fashion and a good purpose"* (33:70)

- Be truthful, do not mix the truth with lie, and hide the
  truth while you know it:

وَلَا تَلْبِسُواْ ٱلْحَقَّ بِٱلْبَٰطِلِ وَتَكْتُمُواْ ٱلْحَقَّ وَأَنتُمْ تَعْلَمُونَ

*"Do not mix truth with falsehood, or hide the truth
when you know it"* (2:42)

- Do not conceal witness:

وَلَا تَكْتُمُواْ ٱلشَّهَٰدَةَ ۚ وَمَن يَكْتُمْهَا فَإِنَّهُۥٓ ءَاثِمٌ قَلْبُهُۥ ۗ
وَٱللَّهُ بِمَا تَعْمَلُونَ عَلِيمٌ

*"Do not conceal testimony (witness); anyone who does so
he has a sinful heart, and God has full knowledge of all that
you do."* (2:283)

Meaning of "speak justly" (*fa'adilu*)

The word *"Adl"* is an abstract noun, derived from verb *"adala"*, which
means: (1) to straighten or to place something in its rightful place; (2)
to be equal or equivalent. In classical Arabic, *"Adl"* denotes: "a
combination of moral and social values indicating fairness, balance,
self-control and straightforwardness" [9].

Justice and fairness are closely related terms that are often used
interchangeably, but there have been distinct understandings of the
two terms. While justice usually has been used with reference to a law
or a rule (i.e. a legal term), fairness has been used to refer to the ability
to judge subjectively without reference to one's feelings or interests
(i.e. a moral term) [9].

The concept of justice in Islam in terms of its political, theological, philosophical, ethical, legal, and economic aspects has been covered extensively in the literatures (Cf. Refs. [10, 11&13]). In this text, dealing with the eighth commandment, the focus is on the establishment of justice as standard of moral excellence for human conduct through speech.

The Quran differentiates between two types of speech, namely the good one and the evil one:

$$أَلَمْ تَرَ كَيْفَ ضَرَبَ ٱللَّهُ مَثَلًا كَلِمَةً طَيِّبَةً كَشَجَرَةٍ طَيِّبَةٍ أَصْلُهَا ثَابِتٌ وَفَرْعُهَا فِى ٱلسَّمَآءِ$$

"Do you not see how God makes comparison? A good word is like a good tree whose root is firm and whose branches are high in the sky." (14:24)

$$وَمَثَلُ كَلِمَةٍ خَبِيثَةٍ كَشَجَرَةٍ خَبِيثَةٍ ٱجْتُثَّتْ مِن فَوْقِ ٱلْأَرْضِ مَا لَهَا مِن قَرَارٍ$$

"And an evil word is like a rotten tree, uprooted from the surface of the earth, with no power to endure" (14:26)

According to Asad [14], the term *kallimah* (word) means any conceptual statement or proposition. Thus, a "good word" describes any idea that is fundamentally true, and it is ultimately beneficial and lasting. Similarly, the "evil word" applies to the opposite of what a divine message aims at, namely to every idea that is essentially false and morally corrupt.

Meaning of "even it concerns a relative" (*wa la' w kana dha qurba*)

To achieve justice, the witness should be more careful in what he or she is saying, particularly *(wa la'w kana)*, if he or she has a close relationship with the offender. Thus, the expression *"dha qurba"* would include relatives from the same family, neighbors, close friends, or any person who is sharing the same racial, cultural, or national background as another.

40

The Significance of the Eighth Commandment

In the Quran

The words "*adl*" and "*qist*" alone recur in the Quran in various forms over fifty times [15]. In addition to the statement of the eighth commandment, the following are examples of similar verses that mandated justice (*adl*) and prohibited injustice (*zulm*):

إِنَّ ٱللَّهَ يَأْمُرُ بِٱلْعَدْلِ وَٱلْإِحْسَٰنِ وَإِيتَآئِ ذِى ٱلْقُرْبَىٰ
وَيَنْهَىٰ عَنِ ٱلْفَحْشَآءِ وَٱلْمُنكَرِ وَٱلْبَغْيِ

"God commands justice, doing good, and generosity towards relatives, and He forbid what is shameful, blameworthy, and oppressive" (16:90)

إِنَّ ٱللَّهَ يَأْمُرُكُمْ أَن تُؤَدُّواْ ٱلْأَمَٰنَٰتِ إِلَىٰ أَهْلِهَا وَإِذَا حَكَمْتُم بَيْنَ ٱلنَّاسِ
أَن تَحْكُمُواْ بِٱلْعَدْلِ

"God commands you to deliver trusts back to their owners, and when you judge between people, you should do that with justice" (4:58)

لَقَدْ أَرْسَلْنَا رُسُلَنَا بِٱلْبَيِّنَٰتِ وَأَنزَلْنَا مَعَهُمُ ٱلْكِتَٰبَ وَٱلْمِيزَانَ لِيَقُومَ ٱلنَّاسُ بِٱلْقِسْطِ

"We sent Our messengers with clear signs, the Scripture and the Balance, so that people could uphold justice" (57:25)

This verse shows that the establishment of justice was the goal of all the revelations and Scriptures. Also, it indicates that justice must be measured and implemented by the standards and guidelines set by the revelations.

In the Sunnah

The following are examples of the Prophet's *hadiths* that ordained justice and forbid injustice:

41

God (*SWT*) spoke through His Messenger in a *hadith qudsi* saying: "O My Servants, I have forbidden injustice for Myself, and forbade it also for you. So, avoid being unjust to one another." (*Muslim*)

The Prophet (*pbuh*) declared in a *hadith* that: "there are seven categories of people whom God will shelter them under His shadows on the Day when there will be no shadow except His; [one is] a just leader (*imam adel*)." (*Muslim*)

The Prophet (*pbuh*) was asked about the great sins. He said: 'they are: to join others in worship with God, to be undutiful to one's parents, to murder a person, and to give a false witness.' The Prophet kept repeating "giving a false witness" with such fervor that we wished he would stop (for his own sake)" (*Al Bukhari*)

Justice with All

1. Justice with God

It is also called the "Great Justice". It is the belief in the Oneness of God, the only supreme power, and the ultimate creator of everything in heavens and the earth. Thus, associating God (*SWT*) with anything in His worshiping, divinity, attributes, power and sovereignty is considered to be a great unjust, because it undermines the true understanding of God:

$$وَمَا قَدَرُواْ ٱللَّهَ حَقَّ قَدْرِهِ$$

"These people have no grasp of God's true measure."
(6:91), (22:74), and (39:67)

In addition, the following acts of wrongdoings are described in the Quran as being a great unjust toward God (*SWT*):

a. Fabricating a lie against God (*SWT*):

وَمَنْ أَظْلَمُ مِمَّنِ ٱفْتَرَىٰ عَلَى ٱللَّهِ كَذِبًا أَوْ كَذَّبَ بِـَٔايَٰتِهِ

*"Who does greater unjust than someone who fabricated a lie
against God or denies His revelations?"*
(6:21), (7:37), (10:17), (11:18), and (18:15)

b. Turning away or refusing God's revelations (signs):

وَمَنْ أَظْلَمُ مِمَّن ذُكِّرَ بِـَٔايَٰتِ رَبِّهِ فَأَعْرَضَ عَنْهَا وَنَسِيَ مَا قَدَّمَتْ يَدَاهُ

*"Who does greater unjust than someone who is reminded of His
Lord's messages and turn his back on them; forgetting all
(the evil) that his hands may have committed?*
(18:57) and (32:22)

c. Spreading doubt about God's revelations:

وَمَنْ أَظْلَمُ مِمَّنِ ٱفْتَرَىٰ عَلَى ٱللَّهِ كَذِبًا أَوْ قَالَ أُوحِيَ إِلَيَّ وَلَمْ يُوحَ إِلَيْهِ شَىْءٌ
وَمَن قَالَ سَأُنزِلُ مِثْلَ مَآ أَنزَلَ ٱللَّهُ

*"Who does greater unjust than someone who fabricated a lie
against Cod, or claims that 'A revelation has come to me', when no
revelation has sent to him, or says: 'I too can reveal something
equal to God's revelation?"* (6:93)

d. Concealing testimony given by God:

أَمْ تَقُولُونَ إِنَّ إِبْرَٰهِۦمَ وَإِسْمَٰعِيلَ وَإِسْحَٰقَ وَيَعْقُوبَ وَٱلْأَسْبَاطَ كَانُواْ هُودًا أَوْ
نَصَٰرَىٰ قُلْ ءَأَنتُمْ أَعْلَمُ أَمِ ٱللَّهُ وَمَنْ أَظْلَمُ مِمَّن كَتَمَ شَهَٰدَةً عِندَهُ مِنَ ٱللَّهِ وَمَا ٱللَّهُ
بِغَٰفِلٍ عَمَّا تَعْمَلُونَ

*"Or do you claim that Abraham, Ishmael, Jacob, and the Tribes
were 'Jews' or 'Christians'? Ask them: 'Do you know more than
God does? And who could be more unjust than someone
who hide a testimony given to him by God?
And God is not unaware of what you do"* (2:140)

43

e. Ruining God's places of worship:

وَمَنْ أَظْلَمُ مِمَّن مَّنَعَ مَسَٰجِدَ ٱللَّهِ أَن يُذْكَرَ فِيهَا ٱسْمُهُ وَسَعَىٰ فِى خَرَابِهَآ أُوْلَٰٓئِكَ مَا كَانَ لَهُمْ أَن يَدْخُلُوهَآ إِلَّا خَآئِفِينَ لَهُمْ فِى ٱلدُّنْيَا خِزْيٌ وَلَهُمْ فِى ٱلْءَاخِرَةِ عَذَابٌ عَظِيمٌ

"Who could be more unjust than those who prohibit the mention of
God's name in His places of worship and strive for their ruin?
Such people should not enter them without fear; there is disgrace for
them in this world and painful punishment
in the Hereafter." (2:114)

2. Justice with Self

To be just with himself, a believer must be aware of the causes of injustice to avoid them, and to ask God's forgiveness and repentance if he committed a speech or an act that is considered unjust. To this end, the Quran identified the following examples as being unjust to the self:

a) Taking partners with God

In Surah *Al-Baqarah* (2:54), Moses (*pbuh*) addressed his people after taking a golden calf as an object of worship in place of God the creator of everything:

وَإِذْ قَالَ مُوسَىٰ لِقَوْمِهِ يَٰقَوْمِ إِنَّكُمْ ظَلَمْتُمْ أَنفُسَكُم بِٱتِّخَاذِكُمُ ٱلْعِجْلَ

"Moses said to his people: 'O my people! Verily, you have sinned
against yourselves by worshipping the calf'" (2:54)

b) Disobeying God's commands

In Surah *Al-a'raf* (7:23), Adam and Eve asked God for forgiveness after disobeying His command by eating from the prohibited tree in Paradise:

قَالَا رَبَّنَا ظَلَمْنَا أَنفُسَنَا وَإِن لَّمْ تَغْفِرْ لَنَا وَتَرْحَمْنَا لَنَكُونَنَّ مِنَ ٱلْخَٰسِرِينَ

"Both of them (Adam and Eve) said:
'Our Lord! We have wronged ourselves,
if You forgive us not, and bestow not upon us
Your mercy, we shall be certainly of the losers.'"
(7:23)

c) Exceeding God's limits

وَمَن يَتَعَدَّ حُدُودَ ٱللَّهِ فَقَدْ ظَلَمَ نَفْسَهُۥ

"Those who overstep God's limits commit unjust
to their own souls" (65:1)

d) Behaving with arrogance and false pride:

وَدَخَلَ جَنَّتَهُۥ وَهُوَ ظَالِمٌ لِّنَفْسِهِ

"And he (the owner of the garden) went into his garden while
in a state of (arrogance) unjust to himself" (18:35)

e) Expressing dissatisfaction with God's blessings:

فَقَالُوا رَبَّنَا بَٰعِدْ بَيْنَ أَسْفَارِنَا وَظَلَمُوا أَنفُسَهُمْ فَجَعَلْنَٰهُمْ أَحَادِيثَ
وَمَزَّقْنَٰهُمْ كُلَّ مُمَزَّقٍ

"They (the people of Sheba) said: "Our Lord has made the distance
between our staging posts so long! They wronged themselves and in
the end, We made their fate a good example, and scattered them to
countless fragments" (34:19)

3. Justice with Mankind

Many aspects of justice with mankind are covered by the Quranic ten
commandments. These included the treatment of orphans covered by
the 6th commandment, dealing fairly with commercial measurements
and transactions discussed in the 7th commandments, and justice in

45

fulfilling contracts and commitments which will be presented in the 9th commandment.

Other examples of justice encouraged by the Quran include the following:

a) Justice in the context of polygamy:

The Quran demands equitable treatment of all wives but as the Quran states:

فَإِنْ خِفْتُمْ أَلَّا تَعْدِلُوا فَوَاحِدَةً

"If you fear that you cannot be just, then marry only one"
(4:3)

b) Justice in the case of divorce:

The Quran instructs the believers not to retain divorced women against their well after completing their waiting-term:

وَإِذَا طَلَّقْتُمُ ٱلنِّسَاءَ فَبَلَغْنَ أَجَلَهُنَّ فَأَمْسِكُوهُنَّ بِمَعْرُوفٍ
أَوْ سَرِّحُوهُنَّ بِمَعْرُوفٍ ۚ وَلَا تُمْسِكُوهُنَّ ضِرَارًا لِتَعْتَدُوا ۚ
وَمَن يَفْعَلْ ذَٰلِكَ فَقَدْ ظَلَمَ نَفْسَهُ

"When you divorce women and they have reached their waiting time, then either retain them in a fair manner, or let them go in a fair manner. But do not retain them against their will in order to harm them; for he who does so, he is being unjust to himself." (2:231)

c) Justice with friends and enemies

God (*SWT*) says:

يَٰأَيُّهَا ٱلَّذِينَ ءَامَنُوا كُونُوا قَوَّٰمِينَ لِلَّهِ شُهَدَاءَ بِٱلْقِسْطِ ۖ
وَلَا يَجْرِمَنَّكُمْ شَنَآنُ قَوْمٍ عَلَىٰ أَلَّا تَعْدِلُوا ۚ ٱعْدِلُوا هُوَ أَقْرَبُ لِلتَّقْوَىٰ ۖ
وَٱتَّقُوا ٱللَّهَ ۚ إِنَّ ٱللَّهَ خَبِيرٌ بِمَا تَعْمَلُونَ

46

*"O' you who believe: be ever steadfast in your devotion to God,
giving witness to the truth in all equity; and never let hatred of any
one lead you to the sin of deviating from justice. Be just: this is the
closest to being God-conscious. And remain conscious of God;
God is aware of all what you do."* (5:8)

God (*SWT*) calls for justice to both friends and enemies which is the
ultimate standard for self-control and compassion. It means that
believers must overlook what happen to them personally, and what
they may have to endure of harm caused by others. In this way, they
give to mankind a great model of moral behavior, and a positive
testimony for Islam.

d)   Justice with Muslims and non-Muslims

God (*SWT*) says:

لَّا يَنْهَىٰكُمُ ٱللَّهُ عَنِ ٱلَّذِينَ لَمْ يُقَٰتِلُوكُمْ فِى ٱلدِّينِ وَلَمْ يُخْرِجُوكُم
مِّن دِيَٰرِكُمْ أَن تَبَرُّوهُمْ وَتُقْسِطُوٓاْ إِلَيْهِمْ ۚ إِنَّ ٱللَّهَ يُحِبُّ ٱلْمُقْسِطِينَ

*"and He does not forbid you to deal kindly and justly to anyone who
has not fought against you for your faith or driven you out of your
homes. God loves those who act equitably."* (60:8)

e)   Justice in resolving internal conflicts

God (*SWT*) says:

وَإِن طَآئِفَتَانِ مِنَ ٱلْمُؤْمِنِينَ ٱقْتَتَلُواْ فَأَصْلِحُواْ بَيْنَهُمَا ۖ فَإِنۢ بَغَتْ
إِحْدَىٰهُمَا عَلَى ٱلْأُخْرَىٰ فَقَٰتِلُواْ ٱلَّتِى تَبْغِى حَتَّىٰ تَفِىٓءَ إِلَىٰٓ أَمْرِ
ٱللَّهِ ۚ فَإِن فَآءَتْ فَأَصْلِحُواْ بَيْنَهُمَا بِٱلْعَدْلِ وَأَقْسِطُوٓاْ ۖ إِنَّ ٱللَّهَ يُحِبُّ
ٱلْمُقْسِطِينَ

*"If two groups among the believers fall to fighting, try to
make peace between them. But if one of them oppresses the*

47

other, then fight the oppressor group until it complies to
God's commandment, then make a just and equitable (even-
handed) settlement between the two of them; God loves those
who are equitable." (49:9)

In his comment on the above verse, Kamali noted the
following [15]:
- Military defeat is not to be used as a means of crushing
  the defeated group.
- All parties are entitled to justice for the sake of gaining
  the pleasure of God.
- The devotion to a cause, country, or people is not a
  valid ground for compromising on justice.
- The nationalist sentiment that is sometimes used to
  justify loyalty at the expense of justice will find little
  support in the Quranic vision of justice.
- Loyalty to one's country is recommended, and so is
  self-exertion and sacrifice for a noble cause, but not if
  these mean compromising on impartial justice.

Guidelines to Speak as a Judge

1. Confirm your Information before Judging

God (*SWT*) says:

وَلَا تَقْفُ مَا لَيْسَ لَكَ بِهِ عِلْمٌ إِنَّ ٱلسَّمْعَ وَٱلْبَصَرَ وَٱلْفُؤَادَ
كُلُّ أُوْلَـٰئِكَ كَانَ عَنْهُ مَسْئُولًا

"Do not follow blindly what you do not know to be true;
Ears, eyes, and heart, you will be questioned
about all these." (17:36)

The Quranic verse prohibits groundless allegations about
events or people, statements based on assumptions
unsupported by evidence, or to get involved in certain
situations that one is unable to evaluate correctly.

Also, refrain from assumptions, as God (*SWT*) says:

يَـٰٓأَيُّهَا ٱلَّذِينَ ءَامَنُواْ ٱجْتَنِبُواْ كَثِيرًا مِّنَ ٱلظَّنِّ إِنَّ بَعْضَ ٱلظَّنِّ إِثْمٌ

*"O' you who believe! Avoid most guesswork (making many
assumptions) as some of the guesswork is sinful"* (49:12)

In the Sunnah, the Prophet (*pbuh*) is reported to say: "Refrain from
assumption, for assumption is the basis of the worst lies".
Accordingly, Islamic law prohibits both the consigning of people to
prison or their manhandling merely on the grounds of suspicion, such
as the use of racial or religious profiling in nowadays.

2. Listen to Both Sides before Judging

A believer should avoid rush judgment and should take his or her time
listening to both sides of a dispute before judging. A Quranic
example from Surah Sad (38:21-26)) is given to demonstrate this
injunction from an episode from the life of Prophet David (*Dawoud*)
(*pbuh*):

وَهَلْ أَتَىٰكَ نَبَؤُاْ ٱلْخَصْمِ إِذْ تَسَوَّرُواْ ٱلْمِحْرَابَ ﴿٢١﴾ إِذْ دَخَلُواْ عَلَىٰ دَاوُۥدَ فَفَزِعَ
مِنْهُمْ قَالُواْ لَا تَخَفْ خَصْمَانِ بَغَىٰ بَعْضُنَا عَلَىٰ بَعْضٍ فَٱحْكُم بَيْنَنَا بِٱلْحَقِّ وَلَا
تُشْطِطْ وَٱهْدِنَآ إِلَىٰ سَوَآءِ ٱلصِّرَٰطِ ﴿٢٢﴾

*"Have you heard the story of the two disputants who climbed the
wall into his (David's) place of worship? He was alarmed in fear
from them as they entered, but they said: 'Have no fear. We have a
dispute: one of us has wronged the other. Judge equitably between
us and do not be partial."* (38:21-22)

The offended party explained his case saying:

إِنَّ هَـٰذَآ أَخِى لَهُ تِسْعٌ وَتِسْعُونَ نَعْجَةً وَلِىَ نَعْجَةٌ وَٰحِدَةٌ فَقَالَ أَكْفِلْنِيهَا
وَعَزَّنِى فِى ٱلْخِطَابِ ﴿٢٣﴾

49

*"This is my brother. He owns ninety-nine ewes, but I own only one.
He says: 'Hand it over to me, and he overpowered me in speech.'"*
(38:23)

David said immediately without listening to the opponent:

قَالَ لَقَدْ ظَلَمَكَ بِسُؤَالِ نَعْجَتِكَ إِلَىٰ نِعَاجِهِۦۖ وَإِنَّ كَثِيرًا مِّنَ ٱلْخُلَطَآءِ
لَيَبْغِى بَعْضُهُمْ عَلَىٰ بَعْضٍ

*"He has certainly wronged you in demanding your ewe in addition
to his ewes. Many partners are often unjust to one another…"*
(38:24)

David soon realized that he made a mistake by rushing into judgment
without listening to the other opponent in the dispute:

وَظَنَّ دَاوُۥدُ أَنَّمَا فَتَنَّٰهُ فَٱسْتَغْفَرَ رَبَّهُۥ وَخَرَّ رَاكِعًا وَأَنَابَ ۩ ﴿٢٤﴾ فَغَفَرْنَا لَهُۥ ذَٰلِكَۖ
وَإِنَّ لَهُۥ عِندَنَا لَزُلْفَىٰ وَحُسْنَ مَـَٔابٍ ﴿٢٥﴾ يَٰدَاوُۥدُ إِنَّا جَعَلْنَٰكَ خَلِيفَةً فِى ٱلْأَرْضِ
فَٱحْكُم بَيْنَ ٱلنَّاسِ بِٱلْحَقِّ وَلَا تَتَّبِعِ ٱلْهَوَىٰ فَيُضِلَّكَ عَن سَبِيلِ ٱللَّهِۚ إِنَّ ٱلَّذِينَ
يَضِلُّونَ عَن سَبِيلِ ٱللَّهِ لَهُمْ عَذَابٌ شَدِيدٌۢ بِمَا نَسُوا۟ يَوْمَ ٱلْحِسَابِ ﴿٢٦﴾

*"David realized that We had been testing him; so he asked his Lord
for forgiveness, fell down on his knees, and repented. We forgave his
misdeed and his reward will be nearness to Us, and a good place to
return to (Paradise). David. We have placed you as a successor on
the earth; so judge fairly between people. Do not follow your desire
for it will divert you from God's path: those who wander from His
path will have painful torment because they forgot the Day of
Reckoning".* (38: 24-26)

Also, in a *hadith* [16], the Prophet (*pbuh*) said to Ali ibn Abi Taleb on
the latter's departure as a judge to the Yemen: 'When the litigants
appear before you, do not decide for one until you hear the other. It is
more likely that by doing so, the reasons for a judgment become clear
to you'.

50

3. Refrain from Following Your Own Desire

يَٰٓأَيُّهَا ٱلَّذِينَ ءَامَنُواْ كُونُواْ قَوَّٰمِينَ بِٱلۡقِسۡطِ شُهَدَآءَ لِلَّهِ وَلَوۡ عَلَىٰٓ أَنفُسِكُمۡ أَوِ ٱلۡوَٰلِدَيۡنِ وَٱلۡأَقۡرَبِينَ ۚ إِن يَكُنۡ غَنِيًّا أَوۡ فَقِيرًا فَٱللَّهُ أَوۡلَىٰ بِهِمَا ۖ فَلَا تَتَّبِعُواْ ٱلۡهَوَىٰٓ أَن تَعۡدِلُواْ ۚ وَإِن تَلۡوُۥٓاْ أَوۡ تُعۡرِضُواْ فَإِنَّ ٱللَّهَ كَانَ بِمَا تَعۡمَلُونَ خَبِيرًا

"You who believe: Be ever steadfast in sustaining justice and bear witness to the truth for the sake of God, even it is against your own selves, your parents, or your close relatives. Whether the person is rich or poor, God can best take care of both. Refrain from following your own desire, so that you can act justly-if you distort or neglect justice, God is fully aware of what you do." (4:135)

This verse provides the following injunctions to achieve and sustain justice:

- The testimony of the believers should not be biased in favor of any of the parties concerned, and should not seek the pleasure of anyone but God (*SWT*).
- To act justly, believers should be in control of their desires and emotions. Thus, believers should not allow the wealth of a rich man to prejudice them in his favor or against him. Similarly, they do not favor a poor man out of compassion, and at the expense of the truth.
- In their entitlement to justice, all people, believers and non-believers, are equal in God's sight.
- We sometime avoid justice when its implementation goes against us or our near ones as we are concerned about protecting our (and their) interests. But God, the All Knower, assures us that He is *'a Better Protector'* of all.
- God, the Most Merciful, reminds us that He (*SWT*) *'is Ever Well-Acquainted with what we do'*. This should enable us to be constantly aware of the Day of Judgment, when we would be standing in front of God (*SWT*) unable to hide any wrong act we might have committed during our life.

51

Summary

- The eighth commandment is focused on the establishment of a standard of moral excellence for human conduct through speech.
- In a just talk, it is preferable to remain silent if you do not know all the facts
- Associating partners with God *(SWT)*, fabricating lies against Him, turning away, and disobeying His divine guidance, spreading doubts about His Scriptures, and destroying His places of worship are considered acts of unjust towards God, and vivid indication that most people have no grasp of God's true measure.
- A believer commits unjust against himself by taking partners with God *(SWT),* disobeying His commands, exceeding His limits, behaving with arrogance, and expressing dissatisfaction with Cod's blessings.
- God *(SWT)* commands justice with all mankind. This includes the believer's family and close relatives, friends and enemies, Muslims and non-Muslims, and in time of peace and time of war.
- God *(SWT)* establishes guidelines for a believer who is appointed or selected to be a judge: to confirm his information and listen to all parties before judging, control his own emotions ad refrain from following his own desires.

References

1. Yusuf Ali, "The Holy Quran: Text, Translation and Commentary", Published in the USA by The Muslim Students Association of the United States and Canada (1975)
2. Sayyid A, Al Mawdudi, "Towards Understanding the Qur'an", translated and edited by Zafar I. Ansari, Published by the Islamic foundation, UK (1988)

3. Pickthall, "The Holy Qur-'aan" (Translation and Transliteration), Published by he Burney Academy, Hyderabad, India (1981).
4. Muhammad T. Al-Hilali and Muhammad M. Khan, "The Noble Qur'an: English Translation of the Meanings and Commentary", Published by King Fahd Complex for the printing of the Holy Qur'an, Medina, K.S.A. (1417 H)
5. Muhammad Asad, "The Message of the Qur'an", (Translation, Transliteration, and Explanations), Published by the Book Foundation, Bristol, England (2003).
6. Sayed Qutb, "In the Shade of the Qur'an", Translated and edited by Adil Salahi, Published by the Islamic Foundation, UK (2006).
7. M.A.S. Abdel Haleem, "The Quran: English Translation and Parallel Arabic Text", Published by Oxford University Press, New York, N.Y. (2010).
8. "Speak a good word or remain silent", ISLAMTODAY.NET,
9. Manuel Velasquez et al, "Justice and Fairness", Article appeared originally in "Issues in Ethics", Vol. 3, No. 2, (Spring 1990), and republished in www.scu.edu/ethics/practicing/decisions/justice.html.
10. Majid Khadduri, "The Islamic Conception of Justice", Published by the Johns Hopkins University Press, London, UK (1984).
11. Hashim Kamali, "Freedom of Expression in Islam" Published by the Islamic Texts Society, Cambridge, UK (1994)
12. Hashim Kamali, "Freedom, Equity and Justice in Islam", Published by the Islamic Texts Society, Cambridge, UK (2002)
13. Maher Hathout et al, "In Pursuit of Justice: The Jurisprudence of Human Rights in Islam", Published by the Muslims Public Affairs Council (MPAC), Los Angeles, Ca. (2006).
14. Ref [6], (14:26) note # 36, p. 376.
15. Ref [11], p. 115.
16. Ref. [11], p. 88

The Ninth Quranic Commandment
"Fulfill your covenant with God"

Meanings of the Words

In Arabic, the ninth Quranic commandment from Surah *Al-An'am* (6:152) reads as follows:

وَبِعَهْدِ اللَّهِ أَوْفُوا

"wa bi ahdil-lahi awfu"

Let us examine the English translation of each Arabic word in this statement:

"wa" means "and", which implies that this ninth commandment is in addition to the previous eight commandments; *"bi"* means "with", *"ahd"* means "covenant"; *"awfu"* is the plural grammatical format of the verb *"waf'fa"* (*n. Wafa'a*) means "fulfill".

Accordingly, the Quranic ninth commandment would be translated as follows:

"And fulfill the covenant of God"

This statement is similar to the English translations of Yusuf Ali [1], Al Mawdudi [2], Pickthall [3], Al Hilali & Khan [4], and Qutb [5]. However, Asad [6] has translated the statement of the ninth commandment as: *"And (always) observe your bond with God"*. He also used the expression "solemn pledge" as synonymous to the word "covenant".

Meaning of Covenant

In the most generic terms, a covenant (in Arabic: *ahd or methaq*) is a binding agreement between two or more parties for the purpose of establishing a mutually beneficial relationship involving obligations and privileges [7].

In religious terms, a covenant denotes a formal agreement between God (*SWT*) and His people, or all mankind at large. Based on this agreement, God promises to guide the people, grant His mercy on them, and give them an eternal place in Paradise. These rewards from God are conditioned upon certain acts on their part, such as worship, obedience, repentance, faith, etc [8]. The people are also warned of dire consequences in case of default. This sort of covenant is an important concept in Judaism, Christianity and Islam [9].

The Importance of Fulfilling Covenants in Islam

- To emphasize the importance of fulfilling covenants, the Quran commanded it repeatedly in several verses such as the following examples:

يَٰٓأَيُّهَا ٱلَّذِينَ ءَامَنُوٓاْ أَوْفُواْ بِٱلْعُقُودِ

"O' you who believe! Fulfill the obligations." (5:1)

وَأَوْفُواْ بِٱلْعَهْدِ ۖ إِنَّ ٱلْعَهْدَ كَانَ مَسْـُٔولًا

"Honor your pledge: you will be questioned about your pledge." (17:34)

وَأَوْفُواْ بِعَهْدِ ٱللَّهِ إِذَا عَٰهَدتُّمْ وَلَا تَنقُضُواْ ٱلْأَيْمَٰنَ بَعْدَ تَوْكِيدِهَا وَقَدْ جَعَلْتُمُ ٱللَّهَ عَلَيْكُمْ كَفِيلًا ۚ إِنَّ ٱللَّهَ يَعْلَمُ مَا تَفْعَلُونَ

"Fulfill any pledge you make in God's name and do not break oaths after you have sworn them, for you have made God your guarantee; God knows everything you do". (16:91)

وَلَا تَشْتَرُواْ بِعَهْدِ ٱللَّهِ ثَمَنًا قَلِيلًا ۚ إِنَّمَا عِندَ ٱللَّهِ هُوَ خَيْرٌ لَّكُمْ إِن كُنتُمْ تَعْلَمُونَ

"And purchase not a small gain at the cost of God's covenant; what is with God is better for you, if you only knew." (16:92)

بَلَىٰ مَنْ أَوْفَىٰ بِعَهْدِهِۦ وَٱتَّقَىٰ فَإِنَّ ٱللَّهَ يُحِبُّ ٱلْمُتَّقِينَ

*"God loves those who keep their pledges and
are mindful of Him."* (3:76)

وَمَنْ أَوْفَىٰ بِمَا عَاهَدَ عَلَيْهُ ٱللَّهَ فَسَيُؤْتِيهِ أَجْرًا عَظِيمًا

*"God will give a great reward to the one who fulfills
his pledge to Him."* (48:10)

- In Islam the fulfillment of covenants is one of the most important
  traits of a true believer as indicated by the following Quranic
  verses:

وَٱلْمُوفُونَ بِعَهْدِهِمْ إِذَا عَاهَدُواْ

*"And (truly pious are) those who keep their promises
Whenever they promise"* (2:177)

وَٱلَّذِينَ هُمْ لِأَمَانَاتِهِمْ وَعَهْدِهِمْ رَاعُونَ

*"And (truly pious are) those who are faithful to their trusts
and to their pledges"* (23:8).

ٱلَّذِينَ يُوفُونَ بِعَهْدِ ٱللَّهِ وَلَا يَنقُضُونَ ٱلْمِيثَاقَ

*"Those who fulfill the agreements they made in God's name and
do not break their covenant."* (13:20)

مِّنَ ٱلْمُؤْمِنِينَ رِجَالٌ صَدَقُواْ مَا عَاهَدُواْ ٱللَّهَ عَلَيْهِ فَمِنْهُم مَّن قَضَىٰ نَحْبَهُ
وَمِنْهُم مَّن يَنتَظِرُ وَمَا بَدَّلُواْ تَبْدِيلًا

*"There are men among the believers who honored their vows
before God: some of them have redeemed their vows by death,
and some of them are still waiting its fulfillment
but they have never changed their decision in the least."*
(33:23).

Types of Covenants

The Quranic covenants have been classified into three basic categories [10]:

1. God's covenants with His People i.e. God's instructions and promises to His human creatures.
2. Human's covenants with God, i.e. man's obligations towards God (*SWT*)
3. Human's covenants among themselves, i.e. between an individual and his fellow-men

The followings are examples of these types of covenants.

1. God's Covenants with His People

The first type of covenant is that between God (*SWT*) and His creatures. We came to know these covenants through the Quranic revelations, and the Prophet's traditions. Examples of this kind of covenants are the following:

a) God's Covenant with Mankind

The first and most honorable covenant is the one that God has taken from each member of the human race during their creation testifying Him to be their Lord. God (*SWT*) says:

وَإِذْ أَخَذَ رَبُّكَ مِنْ بَنِىٓ ءَادَمَ مِن ظُهُورِهِمْ ذُرِّيَّتَهُمْ وَأَشْهَدَهُمْ عَلَىٰٓ أَنفُسِهِمْ أَلَسْتُ بِرَبِّكُمْ قَالُوا بَلَىٰ شَهِدْنَآ أَن تَقُولُوا يَوْمَ ٱلْقِيَٰمَةِ إِنَّا كُنَّا عَنْ هَٰذَا غَٰفِلِينَ أَوْ تَقُولُوٓا إِنَّمَآ أَشْرَكَ ءَابَآؤُنَا مِن قَبْلُ وَكُنَّا ذُرِّيَّةً مِّنۢ بَعْدِهِمْ أَفَتُهْلِكُنَا بِمَا فَعَلَ ٱلْمُبْطِلُونَ

"And when your Lord took out the offspring from the loins (seeds) of the children of Adam, and made them to bear witness about themselves. He said: 'Am I not your Lord? They replied: 'Yes, we bear witness!' So you cannot say on the Day of Resurrection: 'We

*were not aware of this (covenant)' or you say: 'it was our
forefathers who, before us, ascribed partners to God, and we are
only their descendants who followed them: will You destroy us for
the doings of those inventors of falsehoods?"* (7:172-173)

According to this Quranic verse, the ability to perceive the existence
of the Supreme Power is inborn in human nature (*fitrah*). Thus,
knowledge of right and wrong is ingrained in the human conscious,
and therefore, every person is responsible for his actions and will be
fully accountable before God on the Day of Judgment.

b) God's Covenant with His Prophets

God's covenant with all His messengers is to carry out their missions,
to follow His commandments, and to bear witness on their own people
on the Day of Judgment. God (*SWT*) says:

وَإِذْ أَخَذْنَا مِنَ ٱلنَّبِيِّـۧنَ مِيثَٰقَهُمْ وَمِنكَ وَمِن نُّوحٍ وَإِبْرَٰهِيمَ وَمُوسَىٰ وَعِيسَى ٱبْنِ
مَرْيَمَ ۖ وَأَخَذْنَا مِنْهُم مِّيثَٰقًا غَلِيظًا
لِّيَسْـَٔلَ ٱلصَّٰدِقِينَ عَن صِدْقِهِمْ ۚ وَأَعَدَّ لِلْكَٰفِرِينَ عَذَابًا أَلِيمًا

*"We took a solemn pledge from all the Prophets- from you
(Muhammad), from Noah, from Abraham, from Moses, and from
Jesus son of Mary- We took a heavily weighted covenant from all of
them: so that at the end of time, God will question the truthful about
their sincerity, and for those who reject the truth He has prepared a
painful torment."* (33:7-8)

Another covenant of God with the Prophets is to believe and support
Prophet Muhammad (*pbuh*), as God (*SWT*) says:

وَإِذْ أَخَذَ ٱللَّهُ مِيثَٰقَ ٱلنَّبِيِّـۧنَ لَمَآ ءَاتَيْتُكُم مِّن كِتَٰبٍ وَحِكْمَةٍ ثُمَّ جَآءَكُمْ رَسُولٌ
مُّصَدِّقٌ لِّمَا مَعَكُمْ لَتُؤْمِنُنَّ بِهِۦ وَلَتَنصُرُنَّهُۥ ۚ قَالَ ءَأَقْرَرْتُمْ وَأَخَذْتُمْ عَلَىٰ ذَٰلِكُمْ
إِصْرِى ۖ قَالُوٓا۟ أَقْرَرْنَا ۚ قَالَ فَٱشْهَدُوا۟ وَأَنَا۠ مَعَكُم مِّنَ ٱلشَّٰهِدِينَ
فَمَن تَوَلَّىٰ بَعْدَ ذَٰلِكَ فَأُو۟لَٰٓئِكَ هُمُ ٱلْفَٰسِقُونَ

"God took a covenant from the Prophets saying: 'after all the revelations and the wisdom which I have bestowed unto you, there comes to you a messenger confirming the truth already in your possession, you must believe in him and support him. Do you affirm this and accept My covenant as binding on you?' They answered: 'We do.' He said: 'Then bear witness and I shall be your witness'. Those who turn away from this pledge are truly the rebellious."
(3: 81-82)

c) God's Covenant with the Children of Israel

The covenant of God (*SWT*) with the Children of Israel has been referred to in the Quran as "*methaq*" or a strong bond and its commandments are also applied to Christian and Muslim believers:

وَإِذْ أَخَذْنَا مِيثَٰقَ بَنِىٓ إِسْرَٰٓءِيلَ لَا تَعْبُدُونَ إِلَّا ٱللَّهَ وَبِٱلْوَٰلِدَيْنِ إِحْسَانًا وَذِى ٱلْقُرْبَىٰ وَٱلْيَتَٰمَىٰ وَٱلْمَسَٰكِينِ وَقُولُوا۟ لِلنَّاسِ حُسْنًا وَأَقِيمُوا۟ ٱلصَّلَوٰةَ وَءَاتُوا۟ ٱلزَّكَوٰةَ ثُمَّ تَوَلَّيْتُمْ إِلَّا قَلِيلًا مِّنكُمْ وَأَنتُم مُّعْرِضُونَ

"We took a covenant from the Children of Israel: 'Worship none but God; do good to your parents and relatives, to orphans and the poor; speak kindly to all people; keep up the prayers, and pay the prescribed alms (zakat).' Then all but a few of you turned away and paid no attention." (2:83).

2. Human's Covenants with God

The second type of covenant is one that man himself gives to God (*SWT*) in the form of an oath (*Qasam*), or a vow (*Nazr*). These are described briefly in the following sections [11 & 12]:

a) The Oath (*Al Qasam*)

Definition

The Arabic translation for the word "oath" is "*qasam*" or "*yameen*". In Islamic law, an oath is to swear by one of God's names either to affirm the truth of a statement, or to fulfill a promise of doing something, or to abstain from doing something.

An oath must only be made in the name of God (*SWT*) or one of His attributes. This Islamic rule is based on the following Prophet's statements:

- "Whoever wants to take an oath should take it in the name of *Allah* or keep silent" (*Al Bukhari & Muslim*)
- "Whoever swears by other than *Allah* has committed *Shirk (blasphemy)*" (*Ahmad*)
- "Do not swear, except by *Allah*, and do not swear unless you are telling the truth" (*Abou Dawood & An-Nasa'i*).

Thus, taking an oath by anything other than God is prohibited. This includes swearing by the Prophet, the *Ka'bah*, the Quran, spiritual leaders, and the graves of pious people.

It is interesting to note that the use of oath is still common in our society, no matter how secularized it has become, particularly in the west. Most common use of oath is on ceremonial or judicial occasions such as inauguration into office or confirming the truth in court.

Types of Oaths

Classical Islamic jurists have classified oaths into three categories:

1. Sinful Oath (*Al-Qasam Al Ghamus*)

This is when a person intentionally swears to a lie, i.e. committing perjury. It is called "*Al Ghamus*" because it buries the person who does it deep in sin. God (*SWT*) says:

$$\text{إِنَّ ٱلَّذِينَ يَشْتَرُونَ بِعَهْدِ ٱللَّهِ وَأَيْمَـٰنِهِمْ ثَمَنًا قَلِيلًا أُوْلَـٰئِكَ لَا خَلَـٰقَ لَهُمْ فِى}$$
$$\text{ٱلْءَاخِرَةِ وَلَا يُكَلِّمُهُمُ ٱللَّهُ وَلَا يَنظُرُ إِلَيْهِمْ يَوْمَ ٱلْقِيَـٰمَةِ وَلَا يُزَكِّيهِمْ}$$
$$\text{وَلَهُمْ عَذَابٌ أَلِيمٌ}$$

"But those who sell out God's covenant and their own oaths for a trivial gain will have no share in the life to come. God will neither speak to them, nor look at them on the Day of Resurrection, nor will He cleanse them (of their sins); - painful suffering awaits them." (3:77).

Also, the Prophet (*pbuh*) said: "Whoever gives a sinful oath in order to slash part of a man's possessions, he will meet Allah - in the Day of Judgment- angry with him." (*Al-Bukhari and Muslim*).

According to the majority of Juridical Islamic schools, there is no atonement (*Kaffarah*) for a sinful oath, especially if it is related to taking the rights of a person by falsehood. The person committed such a sinful oath must ask God (*SWT*) for forgiveness and sincere repentance.

2. Thoughtless Oath *(Laghw'ul Al Qasam)*

This is the swearing that unintentionally runs upon the tongue of a believer as a sort of speech habit. According to Asad [13], it refers primarily to oaths aiming at denying to oneself something that is not prohibited by Islamic laws. It also applied to all oaths voiced emotionally, e.g. under the influence of anger.

Based on the following Quranic verses, there is no sinful wrongdoing in thoughtless oaths, and there is no obligation of atonement due upon the person who does it:

لَّا يُؤَاخِذُكُمُ ٱللَّهُ بِٱللَّغْوِ فِىٓ أَيْمَٰنِكُمْ وَلَٰكِن يُؤَاخِذُكُم بِمَا كَسَبَتْ قُلُوبُكُمْ ۗ وَٱللَّهُ غَفُورٌ حَلِيمٌ

"God will not call you to account for oaths you have voiced unintentionally but He will call you to account for what you meant in your hearts. God is most forgiving and forbearing."
(2:225)

3. Binding Oath (Al-Qasam Al Mun'aqid)

This is a solemn oath intended to be fulfilled concerning some future matters. The person who breaks the oath is considered accountable, and he or she must compensate for breaking the oath according to the following Quranic verse:

لَا يُؤَاخِذُكُمُ ٱللَّهُ بِٱللَّغْوِ فِىٓ أَيْمَٰنِكُمْ وَلَٰكِن يُؤَاخِذُكُم بِمَا عَقَّدتُّمُ ٱلْأَيْمَٰنَ

"God will not take you (to task) for what is thoughtless in your oaths but only for your binding oaths." (5:89)

In addition, a biding oath should not block any good deed such as an attempt to help the needy, or to establish peace and justice among the people. God (*SWT*) says:

وَلَا تَجْعَلُواْ ٱللَّهَ عُرْضَةً لِّأَيْمَٰنِكُمْ أَن تَبَرُّواْ وَتَتَّقُواْ وَتُصْلِحُواْ بَيْنَ ٱلنَّاسِ
وَٱللَّهُ سَمِيعٌ عَلِيمٌ

"Do not allow your oaths in God's name to hinder you from doing good, being mindful of God, and making peace between people" (2:224).

Accordingly, if one took an oath and later found that it was unintentionally wrong or harmful, he or she should break this oath and give atonement for it. This is based on the following Prophet's Hadith: "By Allah, if anyone of you insists on fulfilling an oath that may harm his family, he commits a greater sin in Allah's concern than that of who breaks up his oath and makes up its atonement with what Allah has commanded." (*Al- Bukhari, vol. 8, Hadith No. 621*).

Atonement of Oath

The atonement (*Kafarah*) for breaking a binding oath is described in the following Quranic verse:

63

لَا يُؤَاخِذُكُمُ ٱللَّهُ بِٱللَّغْوِ فِىٓ أَيْمَٰنِكُمْ وَلَٰكِن يُؤَاخِذُكُم بِمَا عَقَّدتُّمُ ٱلْأَيْمَٰنَ ۖ فَكَفَّٰرَتُهُۥٓ
إِطْعَامُ عَشَرَةِ مَسَٰكِينَ مِنْ أَوْسَطِ مَا تُطْعِمُونَ أَهْلِيكُمْ أَوْ كِسْوَتُهُمْ أَوْ تَحْرِيرُ
رَقَبَةٍ ۖ فَمَن لَّمْ يَجِدْ فَصِيَامُ ثَلَٰثَةِ أَيَّامٍ ۚ ذَٰلِكَ كَفَّٰرَةُ أَيْمَٰنِكُمْ إِذَا حَلَفْتُمْ ۚ وَٱحْفَظُوٓاْ
أَيْمَٰنَكُمْ ۚ كَذَٰلِكَ يُبَيِّنُ ٱللَّهُ لَكُمْ ءَايَٰتِهِۦ لَعَلَّكُمْ تَشْكُرُونَ

*"God will not take you to task for what is thoughtless in your oaths,
but only for your binding oaths. The atonement for breaking an oath
is either to feed ten needy persons with food equivalent to what you
normally give your own families, or to cloth them, or to set free a
slave. But if a person cannot afford that, he should fast for three
days. This is the atonement for breaking your oaths - keep your
oaths. Thus, God makes clear His revelations to you so that you may
be thankful"* (5:89).

According to this verse, the atonement for breaking a biding oath is
one of the following actions;
1. Feeding ten needy persons
2. Clothing ten needy persons
3. Freeing a slave
4. Fasting for three days if a person cannot afford fulfilling
   anyone of the previous actions.

Muslim scholars have different views concerning the interpretation of
these atonement actions such as the type of food or cloth, should and
should not offered to the needy men and women, whether the freed
slave would be a believer or not, and whether the three days of fasting
must be consecutive or not. The details of various scholars' views are
not in the scope of the current text and interested reader may refer to
books of *Fiqh* for details.

b) The Vow (An'*Nazr*)

Definition

A vow is a formal promise made for the sake of God by which a
believer obligates himself or herself to some future act, course of

action, or a way of life that he or she otherwise would not be obligated to do without vowing [11 & 12] .

Types of Vows

1) Permissible Vows

A permissible vow is one that is made sincerely for "the sake of God" alone. They are mentioned in the Quran in approving terms such as in the following examples:

- The vow of Imran's (Amram in the Bible) wife when she was pregnant in Mary:

إِذْ قَالَتِ ٱمْرَأَتُ عِمْرَٰنَ رَبِّ إِنِّى نَذَرْتُ لَكَ مَا فِى بَطْنِى مُحَرَّرًا فَتَقَبَّلْ مِنِّىٓ
إِنَّكَ أَنتَ ٱلسَّمِيعُ ٱلْعَلِيمُ

"Imran's wife said: "O My Lord! I have vowed what is growing in my womb entirely to Your service; so accept this from me. You are the One who hears and knows all." (3:35)

- The vow of virgin Mary after her delivery of Jesus (*pbuh*):

فَإِمَّا تَرَيِنَّ مِنَ ٱلْبَشَرِ أَحَدًا فَقُولِىٓ إِنِّى نَذَرْتُ لِلرَّحْمَٰنِ صَوْمًا
فَلَنْ أُكَلِّمَ ٱلْيَوْمَ إِنسِيًّا

"And say to anyone you may see: 'I (Mary) have <u>vowed</u> to the Most Gracious to abstain from talking and hence I will not talk to anyone today.'" (19:26)

- The pilgrims fulfill their vows before ending their pilgrimage:

ثُمَّ لْيَقْضُوا۟ تَفَثَهُمْ وَلْيُوفُوا۟ نُذُورَهُمْ وَلْيَطَّوَّفُوا۟ بِٱلْبَيْتِ ٱلْعَتِيقِ

"Then let the pilgrims perform their acts of cleansing, fulfill their vows, and circle around the ancient house." (22:29)

2) **Conditioned Vows**:

This type of vow is disliked (*Makrouh*) because it is made conditional for something to happen. For example, a person is saying: "If God cures my illness I shall fast so many days, or I shall give such and such in charity." Such a vow is discouraged by the Prophet (*pbuh*) who said: "Verily, it does not repel anything (i.e. does not change the Divine decree (*qadar*), and it only brings out some of the wealth of the stingy person (i.e. it forces the stingy to give a charity)." (*Al-Bukhari and Muslim*)

3) **Forbidden Vows**

A vow is forbidden (*haram*) when it is vowed for other than Al Mighty God alone. For example, making vows for graves of the righteous people, or the souls of the deceased pious persons is prohibited. This is a form of directing worship to other than God (*SWT*) which is considered to be *Shirk* (associating partners with God); i.e. a violation of the first Quranic commandment: "*Do not associate anything with Him*".

It should be pointed out that a vow is invalid if it was aimed to perform a forbidden (*haram*) or disliked (*makrooh*) act, or to avoid performing a duty (*wajib*) or a desirable (*mustahab*) act. This is due to the Prophet's statement: "There is no vowing in disobedience to God and its atonement is the same as that of an oath." (*Muslim*)

3. Human's Covenants Among Themselves

Covenants among individuals, groups, communities and nations could have a number of forms such as a contract (*Aqd*), a promise (*Wa'd*), a treaty (*Mu'ahada*), and an allegiance (*Bay'ah*). The following is a brief description of these types of covenants from an Islamic perspective.

a) The Contract *(Al Aqd)*

Definition

A contract is an agreement with specific terms between two or more persons or entities in which there is a promise to do something in return for a valuable benefit known as consideration [13].

Contracts are widely used in our daily life. They include sale contracts, loan or mortgage contracts, investment contracts, employment contracts, service contracts, and even social contracts e.g. marriage contracts.

The Basic Elements of an Islamic Contract

The Quran describes the basic elements of an Islamic contract in the following verse (the longest in the Quran) which is dealing with a loan transaction for either an outright loan *(Quard)* or a debt *(Dain)*:

يَـٰٓأَيُّهَا ٱلَّذِينَ ءَامَنُوٓا۟ إِذَا تَدَايَنتُم بِدَيْنٍ إِلَىٰٓ أَجَلٍ مُّسَمًّى فَٱكْتُبُوهُ ۚ وَلْيَكْتُب بَّيْنَكُمْ كَاتِبٌۢ بِٱلْعَدْلِ ۚ وَلَا يَأْبَ كَاتِبٌ أَن يَكْتُبَ كَمَا عَلَّمَهُ ٱللَّهُ ۚ فَلْيَكْتُبْ وَلْيُمْلِلِ ٱلَّذِى عَلَيْهِ ٱلْحَقُّ وَلْيَتَّقِ ٱللَّهَ رَبَّهُ وَلَا يَبْخَسْ مِنْهُ شَيْـًٔا ۚ فَإِن كَانَ ٱلَّذِى عَلَيْهِ ٱلْحَقُّ سَفِيهًا أَوْ ضَعِيفًا أَوْ لَا يَسْتَطِيعُ أَن يُمِلَّ هُوَ فَلْيُمْلِلْ وَلِيُّهُۥ بِٱلْعَدْلِ ۚ وَٱسْتَشْهِدُوا۟ شَهِيدَيْنِ مِن رِّجَالِكُمْ ۖ فَإِن لَّمْ يَكُونَا رَجُلَيْنِ فَرَجُلٌ وَٱمْرَأَتَانِ مِمَّن تَرْضَوْنَ مِنَ ٱلشُّهَدَآءِ أَن تَضِلَّ إِحْدَىٰهُمَا فَتُذَكِّرَ إِحْدَىٰهُمَا ٱلْأُخْرَىٰ ۚ وَلَا يَأْبَ ٱلشُّهَدَآءُ إِذَا مَا دُعُوا۟ ۚ وَلَا تَسْـَٔمُوٓا۟ أَن تَكْتُبُوهُ صَغِيرًا أَوْ كَبِيرًا إِلَىٰٓ أَجَلِهِۦ ۚ ذَٰلِكُمْ أَقْسَطُ عِندَ ٱللَّهِ وَأَقْوَمُ لِلشَّهَٰدَةِ وَأَدْنَىٰٓ أَلَّا تَرْتَابُوٓا۟ ۖ إِلَّآ أَن تَكُونَ تِجَٰرَةً حَاضِرَةً تُدِيرُونَهَا بَيْنَكُمْ فَلَيْسَ عَلَيْكُمْ جُنَاحٌ أَلَّا تَكْتُبُوهَا ۗ وَأَشْهِدُوٓا۟ إِذَا تَبَايَعْتُمْ ۚ وَلَا يُضَآرَّ كَاتِبٌ وَلَا شَهِيدٌ ۚ وَإِن تَفْعَلُوا۟ فَإِنَّهُۥ فُسُوقٌۢ بِكُمْ ۗ وَٱتَّقُوا۟ ٱللَّهَ ۖ وَيُعَلِّمُكُمُ ٱللَّهُ ۗ وَٱللَّهُ بِكُلِّ شَىْءٍ عَلِيمٌ

"O' you who believe! 'Whenever you give or take credit for a stated term, put it down in writing, and have a scribe to write it down justly between you. No scribe should refuse to write; let him write as God has taught him. Let the debtor (i.e. the one who contracts the debt) dictate; and let him be conscious of God, his Lord, and not diminish anything at all from the debt. And if the debtor is weak of mind or

body, or is not able to dictate himself, then, let his guardian dictate justly. And call upon two of your men to act as witnesses. If two men are not available, then call one man and two women out of those you approve as witnesses, so that if one of the two women should make a mistake, the other could remind her. And the witnesses must not refuse whenever they are called upon. And do not be reluctant to write down every contractual conditions, whether small or large, along with the time it falls due; this way is more just in God's sight, more reliable as evidence, and more likely to prevent doubts arising between you. However, if the transaction is a matter of buying and selling on the spot, there is no blame on you if you do not write it down. Have witnesses present whenever you trade with one another, and let no harm be done on either the scribe or the witness, for if you did cause them harm, it would be a crime on your part. Be conscious of God, He teaches you the right way, and God has full knowledge of everything.'" (2:282).

The basic elements of an Islamic contract for a loan or credit as depicted from the above verse are the following:

- The details of all fixed-term contract loans or credits must be recorded in writing, and the time for its repayment should be fixed at the time when the loan is transacted.
- A third party must do the recording to ensure total neutrality and fairness. The writer is required to record the agreed terms of the contract faithfully, without interference, bias or prejudice. He is also obliged to do his job fully and competently as a duty to God who has blessed him with the ability to write.
- The debtor (i.e. the borrower or the party who owes money) is the one who dictates to the writer, acknowledging the amount borrowed, and his commitment to the terms and conditions of the contract as a safeguard against any injustice to him. If the debtor is weak-minded, a minor, or a person unable to dictate because of ignorance, or does not fully understand the business terminology used in such contract, or he is not acquainted with the language in which the contract is to be written, or any other reason, his guardian may do the dictation on his behalf, showing the same quality of accuracy and fairness.

- For the contract to be valid, it must be witnessed by two men, but if these are not readily available, then one man and two women, all of whom are persons of high integrity and enjoying public credibility. The witnesses must not refuse when they are called in and they must carry out their duty willingly, honestly and without any discrimination or prejudice towards either of the parties.
- All debt transactions small or large must be written down in the contract along with all rights and obligations arising from it. Thus, a written contract is seen by God as preferable and fair. In addition, it gives greater force to the testimony of the witnesses since a written statement carries more weight than one based on memory.
- In case of spot trading which normally involving cash transactions rather than credits and executed immediately and frequently, there is no need for written transactions, the mere presence of witnesses will suffice.
- Scribes and witnesses should come to no harm in the course of their obligations towards God, and any wrongdoing they may suffer would be a gross violation to God's law.
- During the entire process, be always conscious of God Who teaches you, and Who has full knowledge of everything.

In principal, the above requirements are applicable to all kind of contracts. However, in each case, it is necessary that the written conditions must be lawful, i.e. within the limits of the Islamic law. For example, a valid Islamic contract cannot involve interest payments or an asset related to a prohibited industry.

For more in depth analysis of Islamic contracts the reader may referto the introductory book on Islamic finance by Jamaldeen [14], or the discussion on the fundamental and theoretical aspects of Islamic commercial contracts by Saleem [15]

b) The Promise (*Al-Wa'd*)

A promise is a declaration or assurance given by one person to another agreeing or guaranteeing to do or to give something in the future.

While a covenant is binding on both parties involved in the contract, a unilateral promise is binding only to one party. To be binding, human unilateral promises may need to be followed by a contract. In these cases, Islamic contract laws are still applied to a unilateral promise, i.e. the person or business making the promise is expected to abide by certain principles and regulations.

Breaking of a promise is a very serious sin as indicated by the following Quranic verse:

فَأَعْقَبَهُمْ نِفَاقًا فِى قُلُوبِهِمْ إِلَىٰ يَوْمِ يَلْقَوْنَهُ بِمَآ أَخْلَفُواْ ٱللَّهَ مَا وَعَدُوهُ وَبِمَا كَانُواْ
يَكْذِبُونَ أَلَمْ يَعْلَمُوٓاْ أَنَّ ٱللَّهَ يَعْلَمُ سِرَّهُمْ وَنَجْوَىٰهُمْ وَأَنَّ ٱللَّهَ عَلَّٰمُ ٱلْغُيُوبِ

"Because they broke their promise to God, because of all the lies they told, He made hypocrisy settle in their hearts until the Day they meet Him. Do they not realize that God knows their secrets and their private discussions? That God knows all that is hidden?" (9: 77-78).

c) The Treaty (*Al Mu'ahada*)

A treaty is a formal written agreement between two or more states in reference to peace, alliance, commerce, or other international agreements [16].

Format

Although a treaty may take many forms, an international agreement customarily includes the following basic elements [17]:
- An introductory statement (preface) gives the names of the parties, a statement of the general aims of the treaty, and a statement naming the persons invested with the power to negotiate the terms of the treaty (plenipotentiaries).
- The substance of the treaty is presented in articles that describe what the parties have agreed upon.
- A statement of the time and place for the exchange of the treaty's ratifications

- A clause at the end of the document that states "in witness whereof the respective plenipotentiaries have affixed their names and seals" and a place for signatures and dates.
- Sometimes additional articles are appended to the treaty and signed by the plenipotentiaries along with a declaration stating that the articles have the same force as those contained in the body of the agreement.

Validation of a Treaty

According to Islamic laws, a treaty must satisfy the following conditions to be validated [17&18]:

- The treaty must not contradict the basic principles of the Quran and the Sunnah. In this respect, the Prophet (*pbuh*) said: "Every condition that has no root in the Quran is void"
- The treaty must be based on the principle of the mutual consent (*redha mota'badel*) of both parties. In Islam, this principle of mutual consent is applied to all contacts or agreements, such as those dealing with trade or reciprocal arrangements, as well as international treaties.
- The treaty must have clear objectives, written in concise and accurate language to guarantee the rights and commitments of all parties involved. As pointed out by the following Quranic verse, deceiving language and ambiguous statements are violation of God's commandments and would lead to failure and evil consequences:

وَلَا تَتَّخِذُوٓاْ أَيۡمَٰنَكُمۡ دَخَلَۢا بَيۡنَكُمۡ فَتَزِلَّ قَدَمُۢ بَعۡدَ ثُبُوتِهَا وَتَذُوقُواْ ٱلسُّوٓءَ بِمَا صَدَدتُّمۡ عَن سَبِيلِ ٱللَّهِۖ وَلَكُمۡ عَذَابٌ عَظِيمٌ

> *"And do not use your oaths to deceive each other lest (in case of) a foot should slip after being firmly placed, and lest (for fear of) you may have to taste the penalty for having hindered others from the path of God, and suffer a terrible torment"* (16:94).

- The treaty must have its designated time which can either be temporary, i.e. limited to a specific time period, or it can be permanent. This condition is explained in a great length by Bsoul [18] and Munir [19].

Termination of a Treaty

A treaty can be terminated under one of the following cases [18]:

1. When its predetermined time period is over.
2. When one party fear treachery from the other party based on clear evidences.
3. When the other side violates any of its essential terms.
4. Changes in circumstances so that the treaty is no longer suites the interest of one or both parties.

The termination of a treaty due to any of the above cases must be publicly announced, and the reasons for the termination must be shared with the other party, so that one is not taken by surprise. This is based on the following Quranic verse:

وَإِمَّا تَخَافَنَّ مِن قَوْمٍ خِيَانَةً فَٱنبِذْ إِلَيْهِمْ عَلَىٰ سَوَاءٍ ۚ إِنَّ ٱللَّهَ لَا يُحِبُّ ٱلْخَآئِنِينَ

"And if you learn of treachery on the part of any people, throw their treaty back at them, for God does not like the treacherous" (8:58).

The Prophet (*pbuh*) further clarified this by saying: "Do not be treacherous even to him who is treacherous to you" (*Abou Dawood*).

d) Allegiance (*Bay'ah*)

Bay'ah is a derivative from the Arabic root *"ba'a"* which denotes both buying and selling. So originally *al bay'ah* was a transaction that is endorsed by hand shaking of the parties involved. In Islamic terminology, *bay'ah* is translated to English as a "pledge of allegiance" to a leader, which was literally translated into Arabic as *"Yameen al walaa"* [21].

The difference between the newly introduced term *"yameen al walaa"* and the traditional *"bay'ah"* may be summarized as follows [21]:

1. The concept of allegiance suggests loyalty of one party to another while *bay'ah* is reciprocal by definition.
2. A pledge of allegiance may be taken in respect to an abstract object (e.g. a nation's flag) or an institution (e.g. the republic), while *bay'ah* must only be given to a qualified individual.
3. An oath is a formal binding commitment in a general way, but in Islam *bay'ah* is sacred, even when no oath is involved.

The above characteristics of *bay'ah* are very well clarified in the following verse:

إِنَّ ٱلَّذِينَ يُبَايِعُونَكَ إِنَّمَا يُبَايِعُونَ ٱللَّهَ يَدُ ٱللَّهِ فَوْقَ أَيْدِيهِمْ ۚ فَمَن نَّكَثَ فَإِنَّمَا يَنكُثُ عَلَىٰ نَفْسِهِۦ ۖ وَمَنْ أَوْفَىٰ بِمَا عَٰهَدَ عَلَيْهُ ٱللَّهَ فَسَيُؤْتِيهِ أَجْرًا عَظِيمًا

"Those who exchange pledges with you (Prophet) are actually exchanging pledges with God - God's hand is placed on theirs- and anyone who breaks his pledge does so to his own loss: God will give a great reward to the one who fulfils his pledge to Him." (48:10)

Thus, in this text we shall avoid translating *bay'ah* as "to give a "pledge of allegiance" and substituting it for "to give a *bay'ah*", or "to exchange *bay'ah*".

Types of *Bay'ah*

Al Mahmoud [22] presented a comprehensive review of different types of *Bay'ah* called for at different times and occasions during the Prophet time, particularly after the establishment of the Islamic state in Medina. The most significant types of *Bay'ah* at this time are the followings:

a) *Bay'ah* of Conversion to Islam:

First and foremost, *bay'ah* denoted conversion to Islam during the life of the Prophet, by stating clearly and unambiguously that "I bear witness that there is no deity but Allah and you (Muhammad) is His

73

messenger". This *bay'ah* was confirmed by grapping the hands of the Prophet with the new convert.

As reported by the Prophet's companions, this *bay'ah* in Islam was sometime combined with some of the basic pillars of Islam such as performing the ritual prayers, giving the alms, listening and obeying, and giving good advice (*nasiha*) to every Muslim (Cf. *Al Bukhari* # 2507)

b) *Bay'ah* of Jihad

Beyond the general commitment to listen and obey, new converts took upon themselves a pledge to defend the new Islamic state by participating in military activities on behalf of God and the Prophet (Jihad in the cause of God). In a variety of contexts, a *bay'ah* was given as a pledge to fight and not to flee (33: 15-16) & (8:15-16), or to fight until death (9:111). The most obvious role of such pledges was to raise the combatants' motivation and fighting spirit in the course of a battle.

c) *Bay'ah* to Establish Islamic Morals

Another example of this kind of *bay'ah* is the one specifically refers to women during the Prophet time, stipulating certain conditions on them if they wish to convert to Islam and enjoy the benefits of being members of the community:

يَـٰٓأَيُّهَا ٱلنَّبِىُّ إِذَا جَآءَكَ ٱلْمُؤْمِنَـٰتُ يُبَايِعْنَكَ عَلَىٰٓ أَن لَّا يُشْرِكْنَ بِٱللَّهِ شَيْـًٔا وَلَا يَسْرِقْنَ وَلَا يَزْنِينَ وَلَا يَقْتُلْنَ أَوْلَـٰدَهُنَّ وَلَا يَأْتِينَ بِبُهْتَـٰنٍ يَفْتَرِينَهُۥ بَيْنَ أَيْدِيهِنَّ وَأَرْجُلِهِنَّ وَلَا يَعْصِينَكَ فِى مَعْرُوفٍ فَبَايِعْهُنَّ وَٱسْتَغْفِرْ لَهُنَّ ٱللَّهَ إِنَّ ٱللَّهَ غَفُورٌ رَّحِيمٌ

"O Prophet! When believing women come and give bay'ah to you that they will not ascribe any partner to God, nor steal, nor commit adultery, nor kill their children, nor lie about who has fathered their children, nor disobey you in any righteous thing, then you should

accept their bay'ah and pray to God to forgive them; God is most forgiving and merciful." (60:12)

According to a number of *Hadiths,* the above *bay'ah* was also used for men converting to Islam to abstain from committing those major sins mentioned in the women's *bay'ah.*

d) *Bay'ah* for Caliphate

A *bay'ah* is an unwritten contract or a pact that involves the recognition of, and giving the *bay'ah* to a *khalifa* (caliph). In essence, it is a commitment from two parties: (1) the *khalifa* i.e the person qualified to be the leader of the Muslim community, and (2) A committee of people who gives him the *bay'ah* pledge. The committee consists of a few numbers of the wise, knowledgeable, and elite members of the community. The *khalifa* commits to adhere to the Quran and the Prophet's Sunnah while the people commit themselves to listen and obey him. The right of the people to revoke the *bay'ah* and rebel against the *khalifa,* if he deviated from his commitment, is being debated by Islamic scholars, and this discussion is beyond the scope of this text.

Consequences of Breaking Covenants

The Quran strongly denounces the breaking of covenants made in the name of God, and described painful torment in Hellfire prepared for those who break their covenants:

ٱلَّذِينَ يَنقُضُونَ عَهْدَ ٱللَّهِ مِنْ بَعْدِ مِيثَٰقِهِۦ وَيَقْطَعُونَ مَآ أَمَرَ ٱللَّهُ بِهِۦٓ أَن يُوصَلَ وَيُفْسِدُونَ فِى ٱلْأَرْضِ ۚ أُوْلَٰٓئِكَ هُمُ ٱلْخَٰسِرُونَ

"Those who break their covenant with God after it has been confirmed, who separate the bonds that God has commanded to be joined, who spread corruption on the earth-these are the losers."
(2:27)

75

وَٱلَّذِينَ يَنقُضُونَ عَهْدَ ٱللَّهِ مِنْ بَعْدِ مِيثَٰقِهِۦ وَيَقْطَعُونَ مَآ أَمَرَ ٱللَّهُ بِهِۦٓ أَن يُوصَلَ وَيُفْسِدُونَ فِى ٱلْأَرْضِ ۚ أُو۟لَٰٓئِكَ لَهُمُ ٱللَّعْنَةُ وَلَهُمْ سُوٓءُ ٱلدَّارِ

"But those who break their confirmed agreements made in God's name, who break apart what God commanded to be joined, and who spread corruption on earth:(as for) those, upon them shall be curse and for them is the evil-terrible home (i.e. Hellfire)." (13:25)

إِنَّ ٱلَّذِينَ يَشْتَرُونَ بِعَهْدِ ٱللَّهِ وَأَيْمَٰنِهِمْ ثَمَنًا قَلِيلًا أُو۟لَٰٓئِكَ لَا خَلَٰقَ لَهُمْ فِى ٱلْءَاخِرَةِ وَلَا يُكَلِّمُهُمُ ٱللَّهُ وَلَا يَنظُرُ إِلَيْهِمْ يَوْمَ ٱلْقِيَٰمَةِ وَلَا يُزَكِّيهِمْ وَلَهُمْ عَذَابٌ أَلِيمٌ

"But those who sell out God's covenant and their own oaths for a small price will have no share in the life to come. God will neither speak to them, nor look at them on the Day of Resurrection, nor will He purify them, and they shall have a painful torment (major suffering in the Hellfire)." (3:77)

إِنَّ شَرَّ ٱلدَّوَآبِّ عِندَ ٱللَّهِ ٱلَّذِينَ كَفَرُوا۟ فَهُمْ لَا يُؤْمِنُونَ ٱلَّذِينَ عَٰهَدتَّ مِنْهُمْ ثُمَّ يَنقُضُونَ عَهْدَهُمْ فِى كُلِّ مَرَّةٍ وَهُمْ لَا يَتَّقُونَ فَإِمَّا تَثْقَفَنَّهُمْ فِى ٱلْحَرْبِ فَشَرِّدْ بِهِم مَّنْ خَلْفَهُمْ لَعَلَّهُمْ يَذَّكَّرُونَ

"The worst creatures in the sight of God are those who reject Him and do not believe. As for those with whom you made a covenant, and who thereupon break their covenant on every occasion, not being conscious of God. If you meet them in battle make of them a fearsome example for those who follow them, so that they may remember." (8:55-57)

Summary

- Covenants covered all commitments and obligations that a human being promised to fulfill, alone or in cooperation with others, for the sake of God's acceptance and love. Fulfilling these covenants

76

is one of the most important moral commandments in Islam that is significantly emphasized in the Quran.

- The most honorable covenant is the one that God (*SWT*) has taken from each human being during his creation, testifying Him to be the only one God to serve, listen and obey.
- Oaths and vows are formal promises made by a human being to God (*SWT*) alone by which he or she is obliged to fulfill sincerely, or in certain cases offers atonement (*kafarah*) for breaking such promises.
- Covenants between people covered by this commandment may have many forms depending upon the specific need of the individual or the group responsible for issuing the covenant. These included contracts, promises, pledges, and allegiances within a Muslim community as well as international agreements, pacts and treaties between nations- both Muslim and non-Muslim.
- This commandment demands truthfulness, accuracy, attention to details, the confirmation of reliable witnesses on written agreements and commitments, and understanding the responsibility and consequences before God regarding contractual agreements and promises.
- This commandment prohibits lying- particularly when under oath, vows made for other than God, deceiving contracts or treaties, acts of treachery against enemies, and discrimination, particularly between Muslim and non-Muslims.

References

1. Yusuf Ali, "The Holy Quran: Text, Translation and Commentary", Published in the USA by The Muslim Students Association of the United States and Canada (1975)
2. Sayyid A, Al Mawdudi, "Towards Understanding the Qur'an", translated and edited by Zafar I. Ansari, Published by the Islamic foundation, UK (1988)
3. " (Translation and Transliteration), Published by the Burney Academy, Hyderabad, India (1981).
4. Muhammad T. Al-Hilali & Muhammad M. Khan, "The Noble Qur'an: English Translation of the Meanings and

Commentary", Published by King Fahd Complex for the printing of the Holy Qur'an, Madinah, K.S.A. (1417 H).

5. Sayed Qutb, "In the Shade of the Qur'an", Translated and edited by Adil Salahi, Published by the Islamic Foundation, UK (2006).

6. Muhammad Asad, "The Message of the Qur'an", (Translation, Transliteration, and Explanations), Published by the Book Foundation, Bristol, England (2003).

7. WordNet search for the definition of the word "covenant" in 68 dictionaries, and T. M. Moore, "*I will be your God*", Phillipsburg, NJ: Presbyterian and Reformed, 2002), 5.

8. www.meeriam-webster.com/dictionary/covenant

9. "The Covenants in the Bible and the Quran- Faith Forum", http://faithforum.wordpress.com

10. Cf. Ref [6], Verse (5:1), note #1.

11. Mahmoud Shaltout, "*Al Fatawa*", Published by Dar Al Shorouk, Cairo, Egypt, the 18th Edition (2004), pp 203-207 (oath); pp 208-212 (vow).

12. Abou Bakr J. Al-Jaza'iry, "*Minhag Al-Muslim*", Vol. No. 2", Published by Darussalam (2001), pp 450 (Oath), pp 457 (Vow).

13. Cf. Ref [6], Verse (5:89), note # 101.

14. Faleel Jamaldeen, "Islamic Finance for Dummies", Published by John Wiley & Sons, Inc., Hoboken, NJ, USA (2008)

15. Muhammad Yusuf Saleem, "Islamic Commercial Laws", Published by John Wiley & Sons, Inc., Hoboken, NJ, USA (2013)

16. http://dictionary.reference.com/browse/treaty

17. http://legal-dictionary.theffreedictionary.com/treary

18. Labeeb A. Bsoul, "International Treaties (*Mu'ahadat*) in Islam", Published by the University Press of America Inc., Lanham, Maryland, USA (2008).

19. Muhammad Munir, "The Concept of Treaty in Relation to War and Peace in Islam", muhammadmunir@iiu.edu.pk

20. Cf. Ref. [2], Vol. IV, verse (16:90), note # 90, pp.358-359

21. Ella Landau-Tasseron, "The Religious Foundations of Political Allegiance: A Study of *Bay'ah* in Pre-Modern Islam", Research Monographs on the Muslim World, Series

No 2, Paper No. 4, May 2010; Hudson Institute, Washington, DC. USA

22. Ahmad Mahmoud Al Mahmoud, *"Al Bay'ah Fil Islam"*, Master Degree Thesis, from Zaytouna University, http://ia600404.us.archive.org/30/items/waq60821/60821.pdf

The Tenth Quranic Commandment
"And this is My Straight Path, then follow it, and do not follow other paths, for they will deviate you from His Path"

Meaning of the Words

In Arabic the tenth Quranic commandment from Surah *Al-An'am* (6:153) reads as follows:

وَأَنَّ هَٰذَا صِرَاطِي مُسْتَقِيمًا فَاتَّبِعُوهُ ۖ وَلَا تَتَّبِعُوا السُّبُلَ فَتَفَرَّقَ بِكُمْ عَن سَبِيلِه

"Wa 'anna hadha sirati mustaqiman-fattabi'uh. Wa la tattabi'us-subula fatafarraqa bikum ann-sabilih."

Let us examine the English translation of each Arabic word in this statement:

"wa" means "and" which implies that this commandment is in addition to the previous nine commandments; *"hadha"* means "this"; *"sirati"* means "My way" or "My path"; *"mustaqiman"* means "straight"; *"fattabi'uh"* means "follow it"; *"Wa la tattabiu"* means "and do not follow"; *"us-subula"(the plural format of the noun "sabeel")* means "other ways"; *"fatafarraqa bikum"* means "for they will deviate you"; *"ann-sabilih."* means "from His way".

Accordingly, the Quranic tenth commandment is translated as follow:

"And this is My Straight Path, then follow it, and do not follow other paths, for they will deviate you from His Path"

This translation of the tenth commandment is consistence with the Quranic translations by Ali [1], Al Mawdudi [2], Pickthall [3], Al-Hilali & Khan [4], Asad [5], Qutb [6], and Abdel-Haleem [7]. The meaning of the words is further analyzed below.

Definition of Terms

"*Al Sirat*" means the road, the way, or the path that provides access to a destination from a source. In this life, our final destination is either Paradise or Hellfire.

"*Al Mustaqeem*" means the straight, i.e. without a bend, angle or curve, but continuing in the same direction without diverting.

"*Al Sirat Al Mustaqeem*" is God's way of proper, honest and moral behavior [8] - the straightway provides the shortest access to our final destination, i.e. Paradise or Hellfire.

In the tenth commandment, *Us-subul (Singl. Al Sabeel)* means roads branched around the Straight Path.

While there is only one Straight Path to God there are multiple of ways (*subul)* that are distracting and deviating from the Straight Path.

Meaning of *"And this is My Straight Path, then follow it"*

The conjunction "and" followed by the pronoun "this" are used in the above sentence to connect the tenth commandment with the nine commandments mentioned in the previous two verses (6:151 and 6:152). Accordingly, the tenth commandment is described as the most comprehensive commandment [9-10], or the mother of all commandments [11], because it combines in itself the entire moral values of Islam. God (*SWT*) is commanding the believers to follow these ethical values because they are His Straight Path (*Siraty Mustaqeeman*) and would lead them to happiness and success in this life and the Hereafter.

Meaning of *"And do not follow other paths, for they will deviate you from His Path"*

At the same time, God (*SWT*) advises the believers not to follow other false paths (in Arabic "*Us-subul*). While there is only one Straight Path to God there are multiple of ways (*subul)* that are distracting the believers and deviating them from God's Straight Path. Thus, these false paths would lead them into failure and destruction in this life and to Hellfire in the Hereafter.

Ibn Masoud reported [12] that one day the Prophet (*pbuh*) drew a straight line. Then, he said: "This is the Path of God". The Prophet then drew lines to the right and to the left of the straight line, and he said: "These are diverse paths and Satan is at every other path signaling towards himself". Then, the Prophet (*pbuh*) recited this verse from surah *Al An'am*:

"This is My Straight Path, then follow it, and do not follow other paths, for they will deviate you from His Path" (6:153)

The Straight Path in the Quran

The subject of the Straight Path has been extensively covered in the Quran. It is presented in more than forty Quranic Surah. The following is a brief summary of the main topics related to the Straight Path:

- **God (*SWT*) is on a Straight Path**

  God (*SWT*) is on a Straight Path has been mentioned twice in the Quran; first time in Surah *Hud*, God (*SWT*) says:

  إِنِّى تَوَكَّلْتُ عَلَى ٱللَّهِ رَبِّى وَرَبِّكُم ۚ مَّا مِن دَآبَّةٍ إِلَّا هُوَ ءَاخِذٌۢ بِنَاصِيَتِهَآ ۚ إِنَّ رَبِّى عَلَىٰ صِرَٰطٍ مُّسْتَقِيمٍ

  "I (Prophet Hud) have placed my trust in God, Who is my Lord and your Lord. There is no moving creature which He does not control. Surely,My Lord is on a Straight Path." (11:56)

  The second time is in Surah *Al Shura*, God (*SWT*) says

  وَإِنَّكَ لَتَهْدِىٓ إِلَىٰ صِرَٰطٍ مُّسْتَقِيمٍ * صِرَٰطِ ٱللَّهِ ٱلَّذِى لَهُۥ مَا فِى ٱلسَّمَٰوَٰتِ وَمَا فِى ٱلْأَرْضِ

*"You (Mohammed) give guide to the Straight Path, the Path of God,
to whom belongs all that is in the heavens and earth"*
(42:52-53)

The verse from Surah *Hud* states that God (*SWT*) has a complete control over all living creatures, and whatever He does is absolutely right. All His actions are rightly directed and sound. None of His actions are random or illogical. The statement *"My Lord is on a Straight Path"* implies that God manages all that is in existence in accordance with a system of truth and justice in the ultimate, absolute sense of these terms [12]. Thus, it is impossible that God (*SWT*) would allow for a conscious evildoer to escape the consequence of his wrongdoing, and He would never let someone with good deeds to go unrewarded, either in this life or in the Hereafter.

In the verse from Surah *Al Shaura*, God (*SWT*) reminded Prophet Mohammad (*pbuh*) that his guidance to his followers through the Quranic revelations is on God's Straight Path.

- **The Prophets were guided to God's Straight Path**

    All God's Prophets, and some of their close relatives, were guided to His Straight Path:

وَكُلًّا فَضَّلْنَا عَلَى ٱلْعَٰلَمِينَ(86) وَمِنْ ءَابَآئِهِمْ وَذُرِّيَّٰتِهِمْ وَإِخْوَٰنِهِمْ وَٱجْتَبَيْنَٰهُمْ وَهَدَيْنَٰهُمْ إِلَىٰ صِرَٰطٍ مُّسْتَقِيمٍ (87)

*"We favored each one of them (the Prophets) over other people,
and also some of their forefathers, their offspring, and their
brothers: We choose them and guided them on
a Straight Path" (6:86-87) (see also (10:89))*

- **God (*SWT*) guides whoever He wills to the Straight Path**

    Addressing Prophet Mohammed (*pbuh*), God (*SWT*) says:

إِنَّكَ لَا تَهْدِى مَنْ أَحْبَبْتَ وَلَكِنَّ ٱللَّهَ يَهْدِى مَن يَشَآءُ ۚ
وَهُوَ أَعْلَمُ بِٱلْمُهْتَدِينَ

"You (Prophet) cannot guide whom you love. But it is God who guides whom He wills; and He is fully aware of those who receive His guidance." (28:56)

God's Messengers showed mankind the Straight Path. A messenger's task is completed when he has made the truth or the straightway clear to people. The output in the form of people following his guidance or going astray is not of his power. It is entirely up to God who has subjected human beings to a law of His own making, in keeping with His free-will. Thus, it is up to the individuals to choose either to follow the Straight Path or not. In both cases, God will guide the individual according to his or her free choice.

Thus, the above verse stresses the inadequacy of human efforts to "convert" any other person to one's own belief or from falling out of the Straight Path, unless that person "wills" to be guided. This fact has been emphasized repeatedly in the Quran (e.g. (2:142), (2:213), (6:39), (10:25), (22:54), (24:46), and (42:52)).

- **The Quran is God's guidance to His Straight Path**

The Quran provides guidance to God's Straight Path, as shown in the following examples:

إِنْ هُوَ إِلَّا ذِكْرٌ لِّلْعَٰلَمِينَ ﴿٢٧﴾ لِمَن شَآءَ مِنكُمْ أَن يَسْتَقِيمَ ﴿٢٨﴾ وَمَا
تَشَآءُونَ إِلَّا أَن يَشَآءَ ٱللَّهُ رَبُّ ٱلْعَٰلَمِينَ ﴿٢٩﴾

"This (Quran) is no less than a reminder for the Worlds. For whoever of you wishes to be straight. And you cannot will anything except if God also wills, the Lord of all the worlds." (81: 27-29)

85

وَهَٰذَا صِرَٰطُ رَبِّكَ مُسْتَقِيمًا ۗ قَدْ فَصَّلْنَا ٱلْءَايَٰتِ لِقَوْمٍ يَذَّكَّرُونَ

*"And this (Quran) is your Lord's Straight Path. We have
fully detailed the revelations to those who remember."*
(6:126)

الٓر ۚ كِتَٰبٌ أَنزَلْنَٰهُ إِلَيْكَ لِتُخْرِجَ ٱلنَّاسَ مِنَ ٱلظُّلُمَٰتِ إِلَى ٱلنُّورِ بِإِذْنِ
رَبِّهِمْ إِلَىٰ صِرَٰطِ ٱلْعَزِيزِ ٱلْحَمِيدِ

*"Alif Lam Ra, this (Quran) is a Scripture that We have sent
to you (Prophet) so that, with your Lord's permission, you
may bring people from the depths of darkness into light, to
the Path of the All-Mighty, the Praiseworthy one"* (14:1)

- **The true believers are on God's Straight Path**

The Straight Path is the path of the blessed believers who are
described in Surah *Al- Fatiha* as being:

صِرَٰطَ ٱلَّذِينَ أَنْعَمْتَ عَلَيْهِمْ غَيْرِ ٱلْمَغْضُوبِ عَلَيْهِمْ وَلَا ٱلضَّآلِّينَ

*"The path of those You (God) have blessed, those who did not
acquire Your anger,
and those who have not gone astray"* (1:7)

In addition, the Quran identifies the blessed followers as a
distinguished group who obey God and the Messenger, and
therefore stand firm on God's Straight Path:

وَمَن يُطِعِ ٱللَّهَ وَٱلرَّسُولَ فَأُو۟لَٰٓئِكَ مَعَ ٱلَّذِينَ أَنْعَمَ ٱللَّهُ عَلَيْهِم مِّنَ ٱلنَّبِيِّۦۧنَ
وَٱلصِّدِّيقِينَ وَٱلشُّهَدَآءِ وَٱلصَّٰلِحِينَ ۚ وَحَسُنَ أُو۟لَٰٓئِكَ رَفِيقًا

*"Whoever obeys God and the Messenger will be among those He
has blessed: the messengers, the truthful, the martyrs, and the
righteous- what excellent companions
these are!"* (4:69)

This distinguished group consists of the following four categories:

1. The Messengers who get inspirations from God, and who teach mankind by example and through the implementation of God's commandments, and rules of conduct.

2. The truthful (*Al Siddiqeen*) who are extremely honest, always sincere and straight forward, when dealing with others. They support, and defend whatever is truthful, and they do not waiver in their opposition to falsehood.

3. The witnesses (*Al Shohood*) which means those who testify to the truth, and they acquire high level of good reputation that their testimony, on any matter, is accepted without hesitation. *Al Shaheed is* also means the "martyrs", those who are willing to scarify their own life fighting in a just war for the cause of God.

4. The righteous (*Al Saliheen*) who are the believers and whose entire life has been oriented toward righteousness, i.e. with great concern of morals and ethics.

- **The Straight Path is the Path of Moderation (*Al Wasatiyah*)**

يَهْدِى مَن يَشَآءُ إِلَىٰ صِرَٰطٍ مُّسْتَقِيمٍ * وَكَذَٰلِكَ جَعَلْنَٰكُمْ أُمَّةً وَسَطًا لِّتَكُونُواْ شُهَدَآءَ عَلَى ٱلنَّاسِ وَيَكُونَ ٱلرَّسُولُ عَلَيْكُمْ شَهِيدًا

"He (God) guides whomever He wills to a Straight Path.
"Thus, We have made you a mid-way community, so that you might bear witness to the truth before the rest of mankind, and the Messenger might bear witness to it before you" (2:142-143)

Islam endorses moderation and balance in everything including belief, worship, conduct, transactions, and legislations [14]. Moderation also means the straightness of the conduct and avoiding the tendency toward crookedness and deviation. So, if one assumes many lines connecting two opposite points, then the straight line would be the shortest line located in the middle of these deviated lines. As such, Islamic texts [15] call upon Muslims to exercise moderation and to reject all kinds of extremist paths such as the following:

- *"Ghuluw"* or *"ifrat"* means exceeding the limits or excessiveness. The expression *"wa la-taghluw fi deanikum"* stated in the Quran and *"iyakum wa al-ghuluw fi al-dean"* mentioned in the Prophetic traditions, both exceeding the proper bound or extremism. For example, one goes beyond the limits if he makes unlawful things lawful or abstains from things which God has allowed.

    "Jafa" or *"tashdid"* means harshness, roughness, antipathy, aversion or alienation. Examples of *"jafa"* include mistreatment of parents, rudeness or impoliteness in human relations, and disconnecting relationship with kin and relatives.

The Straight Path is to follow God's Commandments

God's commandments, as depicted from Surah *Al An'am* verses (6:151-153), provide the core moral values and the standard of appropriate behavior. These constitute God's Straight Path for the Muslim community. To recap, these are the followings:

1. It is God's Straight Path that defines the relationship between man and his creator based on absolute monotheism, complete submission to the will of God, unparalleled love, and total trust in Him.
2. It is God's Straight Path that mandates goodness to parents by seeking perfection in every deed, act or say to them. It prohibits any kind of abuse to parents and considers such act a major sin.
3. It is God's Straight Path that recognizes the humanity of a child before and after his or her birth, and commands that his or her life deserves respect and protection at all stages of his or her development.
4. It is God's Straight Path that emphasizes purity, decency, and chastity as the foundation of the faithful family. Hence, it

forbids all shameful deeds related to sexual relationships outside the legal marriage bond between a man and a woman.

5. It is God's Straight Path that stresses the scanty of human life and forbids taking its soul except for a just divine cause defined by the Islamic law. It does not allow absolute freedom to the individuals to act like beasts who destroy and kill, and control the weak, and the helpless in the society. At the same time, it ordains saving human life that otherwise could be destroyed due to poverty, hunger, diseases, and/or ignorance.

6. It is God's Straight Path that emphasizes social justice and merciful treatment of orphans, the weakest elements in society. It establishes a system of orphans' sponsorship (*kafalah)* that is managed by an appointed guardian until the orphan reaches the age of maturity.

7. It is God's Straight Path to conduct commercial deals based on the moral values of honesty, trustworthiness, leniency, justice, and the continuous remembrance of God. In addition, it prohibits business practices based on usury, price fixing, hoarding, deceptive transactions, bribery and dealing with unlawful items, such as alcoholic drinks and pork meat.

8. It is God's Straight Path to achieve justice with all mankind. This includes a believer's own family, close relatives, friends and enemies, men and women, Muslims and non-Muslims, and in times of peace or wars. Thus, before judging, a God conscious judge must confirm his information, listen to all parties, control his emotions, and refrain from his own biases and whims.

9. It is God's Straight Path to fulfil our covenants to Him, to ourselves, to our community, and to other nations. God does not accept for His followers the life of weakness, oppression, and surrender. Also, He does not accept for them a life of injustice, destruction, and terrorism.

In addition, God's Straight Path as defined by His commandments provides a navigation tool, a set of criteria to assess where we actually are and where we ought to be going in the path of our life's journey.

This should take each aspect of a believer's life at a mid-way position away from corrupted or extremists' views.

Straightness

Straightness means continuous progression towards a target without any doubt or hesitation [16]. In Islam, straightness ("*Istiqamah*" in Arabic) means to stand firm on the Straight Path of God without any deviation, and perform all that was ordained, and abstain from all that was forbidden [17-19]. In addition, a believer must be conscious not to overstep the bounds or exceed the limits of what God has ordained or prohibited. Indeed, straightness is a very difficult task to achieve and maintain.

Despite the fact that Prophet Mohammad (*pbuh*) was the best model of human morality, he was commanded along with his followers, to keep firm stand on the Straight Path, as God (*SWT*) says:

فَٱسْتَقِمْ كَمَآ أُمِرْتَ وَمَن تَابَ مَعَكَ وَلَا تَطْغَوْاۚ إِنَّهُۥ بِمَا تَعْمَلُونَ بَصِيرٌ

"Stand firm on the Straight Path of God as you are commanded and those who turn in repentance with you, and do not exceed your limits, God is All-aware of everything they do"
(11:112) (Also see (42:15) and (41:6))

The Prophet (*pbuh*) felt the power behind this order and the significance of its responsibility. He was reported to have said: "This surah (*Hud*), has made my hair grow grey." Here the Prophet is commanded (along with his followers) to maintain the Straight Path without any deviation. This requires him to be always alert, careful, watchful, and aware of his path. He was also known to be in full control of his emotions and feelings.

Attaining Straightness

- Strive for sincerity in serving God (*SWT*) alone. God (*SWT*) says:

وَمَا أُمِرُوا إِلَّا لِيَعْبُدُوا اللَّهَ مُخْلِصِينَ لَهُ الدِّينَ حُنَفَاءَ وَيُقِيمُوا الصَّلَاةَ وَيُؤْتُوا الزَّكَاةَ ۚ وَذَلِكَ دِينُ الْقَيِّمَةِ

*"though all they commanded to do was worship God alone,
sincerely devoting their religion to Him as people of true faith, keep
up the prayers and pay the prescribed alms, for that is the true
religion"* (98:5)

- Conduct soul-searching through deep and critical examination of one's motives, actions, conventions, and attitudes. Soul searching is required as indicated by the following verse:

يَـٰٓأَيُّهَا ٱلَّذِينَ ءَامَنُوا۟ ٱتَّقُوا۟ ٱللَّهَ وَلْتَنظُرْ نَفْسٌ مَّا قَدَّمَتْ لِغَدٍ

*"O' you who believe! Remain conscious of God and let every
human soul look carefully what it has put forth for tomorrow"*
(59:18)

So the purpose of soul searching is to examine the readiness of God's servant to stand before Him in the Day of Judgment.

- Keep continuous connection with God through prayers. In addition to being an expression of thankfulness to God and appreciation of Him, prayers are safeguards against indecency and corruption. God (*SWT*) says:

ٱتْلُ مَآ أُوحِىَ إِلَيْكَ مِنَ ٱلْكِتَـٰبِ وَأَقِمِ ٱلصَّلَوٰةَ ۖ إِنَّ ٱلصَّلَوٰةَ تَنْهَىٰ عَنِ ٱلْفَحْشَآءِ وَٱلْمُنكَرِ ۗ وَلَذِكْرُ ٱللَّهِ أَكْبَرُ ۗ وَٱللَّهُ يَعْلَمُ مَا تَصْنَعُونَ

*"Recite what has been revealed to you of the Scripture, keep
up the prayers. Prayer restrains shameful and evil deeds,
and remembrance of God is indeed the greatest deed, and
God knows all what you do"* (29:45)

- Choose righteous friends because such companions will help one serving God, fulfilling His commandments, and seeking His knowledge. God (*SWT*) says:

وَٱصْبِرْ نَفْسَكَ مَعَ ٱلَّذِينَ يَدْعُونَ رَبَّهُم بِٱلْغَدَوٰةِ وَٱلْعَشِيِّ يُرِيدُونَ وَجْهَهُۥ وَلَا تَعْدُ عَيْنَاكَ عَنْهُمْ تُرِيدُ زِينَةَ ٱلْحَيَوٰةِ ٱلدُّنْيَا وَلَا تُطِعْ مَنْ أَغْفَلْنَا قَلْبَهُۥ عَن ذِكْرِنَا وَٱتَّبَعَ هَوَىٰهُ وَكَانَ أَمْرُهُۥ فُرُطًا

"And keep yourself patiently with those who call for their Lord, morning and evening, seeking His pleasure, and do not let your eyes overlook them, desiring the attractions of this worldly life. And do not obey him whose heart We have made heedless of Our remembrance, and who follows his own desires and his fate was lost." (18:28)

Consequences of Straightness

God (*SWT*) says:

إِنَّ ٱلَّذِينَ قَالُوا۟ رَبُّنَا ٱللَّهُ ثُمَّ ٱسْتَقَٰمُوا۟ تَتَنَزَّلُ عَلَيْهِمُ ٱلْمَلَٰئِكَةُ أَلَّا تَخَافُوا۟ وَلَا تَحْزَنُوا۟ وَأَبْشِرُوا۟ بِٱلْجَنَّةِ ٱلَّتِي كُنتُمْ تُوعَدُونَ ﴿٣٠﴾ نَحْنُ أَوْلِيَآؤُكُمْ فِى ٱلْحَيَوٰةِ ٱلدُّنْيَا وَفِى ٱلْءَاخِرَةِ وَلَكُمْ فِيهَا مَا تَشْتَهِىٓ أَنفُسُكُمْ وَلَكُمْ فِيهَا مَا تَدَّعُونَ ﴿٣١﴾

"Those who say: 'Our Lord is God' and then stand firm on His Straight Path, the angels descend to them and say: 'Have no fear or grief, but rejoice in the good news of Paradise which you have been promised. We are your allies in this world and in the Hereafter, where you will have everything you desire and ask for as a welcoming gift from the Most Forgiving, the Most Merciful'".
(41:30-31) (also see (46:13-14))

From this verse, we could summarize the benefits of straightness as follow:
- Peace in heart due to continuous connection to God (*SWT*)
- No fear about what is coming and no sadness about whatever is lost
- The love, the respect, and the appreciations of the people around them because of their good manners and their sincere obedience.
- God promises them Paradise in the Hereafter

Causes of Deviation from God's Straight Path

1. Lack of Determination

A determined person is decisive and has self-control. Thus, through patience and determination, he is capable of fulfilling his commitments, preserving his covenants, and staying on the Straight Path. In the following verse, God (*SWT*) attributes the causes of Prophet Adam's failure in keeping his covenant were his forgetfulness and his lack of determination:

وَلَقَدْ عَهِدْنَآ إِلَىٰ ءَادَمَ مِن قَبْلُ فَنَسِىَ وَلَمْ نَجِدْ لَهُ عَزْمًا

"We also commanded Adam before you, but he forgot and We found no firmness of purpose in him)." (20:115)

Lack of determination could also be related to lack of freedom or the dependence on others to control one's life, as illustrated by the following Quranic verses:

ضَرَبَ ٱللَّهُ مَثَلًا عَبْدًا مَّمْلُوكًا لَّا يَقْدِرُ عَلَىٰ شَىْءٍ وَمَن رَّزَقْنَـٰهُ مِنَّا رِزْقًا حَسَنًا فَهُوَ يُنفِقُ مِنْهُ سِرًّا وَجَهْرًا ۚ هَلْ يَسْتَوُۥنَ ۚ ٱلْحَمْدُ لِلَّهِ ۚ بَلْ أَكْثَرُهُمْ لَا يَعْلَمُونَ

"God presents the parable of a slave controlled by his master, with no power over anything, and another man We have supplied with good provisions, from which he gives alms privately and openly. Can they be considered equal? All praises belong to God, but most of them do not recognize this" (16:75)

وَضَرَبَ ٱللَّهُ مَثَلًا رَّجُلَيْنِ أَحَدُهُمَآ أَبْكَمُ لَا يَقْدِرُ عَلَىٰ شَىْءٍ وَهُوَ كَلٌّ عَلَىٰ مَوْلَىٰهُ أَيْنَمَا يُوَجِّههُّ لَا يَأْتِ بِخَيْرٍ ۖ هَلْ يَسْتَوِى هُوَ وَمَن يَأْمُرُ بِٱلْعَدْلِ ۙ وَهُوَ عَلَىٰ صِرَٰطٍ مُّسْتَقِيمٍ

"God presents the parable of two men, one of them dumb, unable to do anything, a burden on his caregiver-whatever task he directs him

to, he achieves nothing good- can he be considered equal to one
who commands justice and is on the Straight Path?
(16:76)

2. Forgetfulness

The following Quranic verses indicate that intentional forgetfulness of God (*SWT*) leads to the forgetfulness of oneself and the deviation from God's Straight Path:

وَلَا تَكُونُواْ كَٱلَّذِينَ نَسُواْ ٱللَّهَ فَأَنسَىٰهُمْ أَنفُسَهُمْ ۚ أُوْلَـٰٓئِكَ هُمُ ٱلْفَـٰسِقُونَ

"And do not be like those who forget God, so God causes them to
forget their own souls; they are the rebellious ones." (59:19)

فَبِمَا نَقْضِهِم مِّيثَـٰقَهُمْ لَعَنَّـٰهُمْ وَجَعَلْنَا قُلُوبَهُمْ قَـٰسِيَةً ۖ يُحَرِّفُونَ ٱلْكَلِمَ عَن مَّوَاضِعِهِۦ ۙ
وَنَسُواْ حَظًّا مِّمَّا ذُكِّرُواْ بِهِۦ ۚ

"Because they broke theirs covenant, We cursed them and made
their hearts grow hard. They distort the meaning of (revealed)
words and have forgotten some of what they were told to
remember..." (5:13)

3. Hypocrisy

A hypocrite is someone who says one thing and does the opposite. According to the following verse, such a trait is the most hateful to God (*SWT*) as it deviates people from His Straight Path:

يَـٰٓأَيُّهَا ٱلَّذِينَ ءَامَنُواْ لِمَ تَقُولُونَ مَا لَا تَفْعَلُونَ
كَبُرَ مَقْتًا عِندَ ٱللَّهِ أَن تَقُولُواْ مَا لَا تَفْعَلُونَ

"O' you who believe: Why do you say things and then do not do
them? It is most hateful to God that you say things and then do not
do them." (61:2-3)

An example of a hypocrite behavior is shown in the following Quranic verses:

وَمِنْهُم مَّنْ عَٰهَدَ ٱللَّهَ لَئِنْ ءَاتَىٰنَا مِن فَضْلِهِۦ لَنَصَّدَّقَنَّ وَلَنَكُونَنَّ مِنَ ٱلصَّٰلِحِينَ

فَلَمَّآ ءَاتَىٰهُم مِّن فَضْلِهِۦ بَخِلُواْ بِهِۦ وَتَوَلَّواْ وَّهُم مُّعْرِضُونَ

فَأَعْقَبَهُمْ نِفَاقًا فِى قُلُوبِهِمْ إِلَىٰ يَوْمِ يَلْقَوْنَهُۥ بِمَآ أَخْلَفُواْ ٱللَّهَ مَا وَعَدُوهُ

وَبِمَا كَانُواْ يَكْذِبُونَ

"And there are those of them who made a covenant with God, saying: 'If He gives us out of His grace, we will certainly give alms and we will be certainly among those who are righteous.' Then, when He did give them out of His grace, they become miserly and turned stubbornly away. Because they broke their covenant with God, because of all the lies they told, He made hypocrisy settled in their hearts until the Day they meet Him" (9:75-77)

4. Satanic Temptations

Since the creation of the first man (Adam), Satan has been determined to corrupt human beings, and drifting them away from God's Straight Path, except those who are devoted believers. God (*SWT)* says [Cf. (2:30), (4:116), and (7:11)]:

قَالَ رَبِّ فَأَنظِرْنِىٓ إِلَىٰ يَوْمِ يُبْعَثُونَ

قَالَ فَإِنَّكَ مِنَ ٱلْمُنظَرِينَ

إِلَىٰ يَوْمِ ٱلْوَقْتِ ٱلْمَعْلُومِ

قَالَ رَبِّ بِمَآ أَغْوَيْتَنِى لَأُزَيِّنَنَّ لَهُمْ فِى ٱلْأَرْضِ وَلَأُغْوِيَنَّهُمْ أَجْمَعِينَ

إِلَّا عِبَادَكَ مِنْهُمُ ٱلْمُخْلَصِينَ

قَالَ هَٰذَا صِرَٰطٌ عَلَىَّ مُسْتَقِيمٌ

إِنَّ عِبَادِى لَيْسَ لَكَ عَلَيْهِمْ سُلْطَٰنٌ إِلَّا مَنِ ٱتَّبَعَكَ مِنَ ٱلْغَاوِينَ

وَإِنَّ جَهَنَّمَ لَمَوْعِدُهُمْ أَجْمَعِينَ

"Iblis (Satan) said: 'My Lord, give me respite (relief) until the Day when they will be resurrected'. God answered: 'You are granted respite, until the Day of the Appointed Time.' Iblis then said: 'Because You have put me in the wrong, I will lure mankind on

Earth and put them in the wrong; all except Your devoted servants'
God said: 'Devotion is a Straight Path to Me; you will have no
power over My servants, only over the ones who go astray and
follow you. And surely Hell is the promised place for them all.'"
(15:36-43)

Accordingly, those who follow the footsteps of Satan will deviate from God's Straight Path, and will be guided to the road of Hellfire.

Forms of Deviation from God's Straight Path

According to the tenth commandment, while there is only one Straight Path to God there are multiple ways that are distracting and deviating from the Straight Path. This section describes some of these paths of deviation that are challenging the believers.

1. Intellectualism

Although most people confess a nominal faith in God, some intellectuals are taking a skeptical attitude (doubt, distrust, disbelief, etc....) using philosophical theories and metaphysical speculations [20], to deviate believers from God's Straight Path. These include the following philosophical concepts:
- Atheism: the philosophy that there is no God.
- Relativism: a popular point of view which states that absolute truth does not exist.
- Hedonism: a philosophy which holds that man's chief and highest goal is pleasure.
- Universalism: the claim that denies the reality of eternal punishment and postulates the eventual salvation of all.

The Quran establishes the essential requirements for true believers, those who have total trust in God. Specifically, the Quran states the following conditions as prerequisites to receive God's guidance that leads to His Straight Path:

ذَٰلِكَ ٱلْكِتَٰبُ لَا رَيْبَ ۛ فِيهِ ۛ هُدًى لِّلْمُتَّقِينَ ﴿٢﴾ ٱلَّذِينَ يُؤْمِنُونَ بِٱلْغَيْبِ وَيُقِيمُونَ ٱلصَّلَوٰةَ وَمِمَّا رَزَقْنَٰهُمْ يُنفِقُونَ ﴿٣﴾ وَٱلَّذِينَ يُؤْمِنُونَ بِمَآ أُنزِلَ إِلَيْكَ وَمَآ أُنزِلَ مِن قَبْلِكَ وَبِٱلْءَاخِرَةِ هُمْ يُوقِنُونَ ﴿٤﴾ أُوْلَٰئِكَ عَلَىٰ هُدًى مِّن رَّبِّهِمْ ۖ وَأُوْلَٰئِكَ هُمُ ٱلْمُفْلِحُونَ ﴿٥﴾

"This book (the Quran)-let there be no doubt about it- is a guidance for all the God conscious. Those who believe in the existence of that which is beyond the reach of human perception, who establish prayers, and spend out of what We have provided to them. Who believe in what has been revealed to you and what was revealed before you, and have firm faith in the Hereafter. Such people are on true guidance from their Lord, those who are the truly successful*

(2: 2-5)

Thus, the above verses defined the conditions for a person to receive God's guidance to His Straight Path as follow:

1) To believe in the *ghayb, which* signifies the subjects or phases of reality that are beyond the scope of human's perception, and cannot, therefore, be proved or disproved by scientific observations and methodologies. Examples of *ghayb* are the existence and attributes of God, the angels, the revelation process, life- after-death, Paradise, Hell, and so on.

2) To establish regular prayers, which are continuing sign of practical obedience, and devoting connection to God (*SWT*).

3) To spend on others from what God has provided them (*Ar-rizq*), which applies to all that may be beneficial to man such as food and knowledge.

4) To believe in the book revealed to Prophet Muhammed (*pbuh*) i.e. the Quran, as well as in those divine books revealed to other Prophets who preceded him, such as the Torah, and the Gospel.

5) To believe without any doubt in the Hereafter when every human being will be resurrected and questioned by God regarding all his conducts in this world. Those who are accounted with good deeds in God's judgement will be sent to Paradise, and those judged by Him as evil doers will be consigned to Hell.

Those who are in a state of doubt and hesitation with regard to these five conditions- let alone disbelieving them- could not attain even one step forward on God's Straight Path:

وَمَن يَكْفُرْ بِٱللَّهِ وَمَلَـٰئِكَتِهِ وَكُتُبِهِ وَرُسُلِهِ وَٱلْيَوْمِ ٱلْـَٔاخِرِ فَقَدْ ضَلَّ ضَلَـٰلًۢا بَعِيدًا

"And he who denies God, His angels, His revelations, His messengers, and the Last Day, has indeed gone far astray"
(4:136)

God (*SWT*) declared that such people are the most to fail by their actions:

قُلْ هَلْ نُنَبِّئُكُم بِٱلْأَخْسَرِينَ أَعْمَـٰلًا ﴿١٠٣﴾ ٱلَّذِينَ ضَلَّ سَعْيُهُمْ فِى ٱلْحَيَوٰةِ ٱلدُّنْيَا وَهُمْ يَحْسَبُونَ أَنَّهُمْ يُحْسِنُونَ صُنْعًا ﴿١٠٤﴾ أُولَـٰئِكَ ٱلَّذِينَ كَفَرُواْ بِـَٔايَـٰتِ رَبِّهِمْ وَلِقَآئِهِ فَحَبِطَتْ أَعْمَـٰلُهُمْ فَلَا نُقِيمُ لَهُمْ يَوْمَ ٱلْقِيَـٰمَةِ وَزْنًا ﴿١٠٥﴾ ذَٰلِكَ جَزَآؤُهُمْ جَهَنَّمُ بِمَا كَفَرُواْ وَٱتَّخَذُوٓاْ ءَايَـٰتِى وَرُسُلِى هُزُوًا ﴿١٠٦﴾

"Say: Shall We tell you who are the greatest losers in whatever they may do? "It is they whose effort has gone astray in this world, and who nonetheless think that what they do is right. It is they who have chosen to deny their Lord's revelations, and the truth that they will meet Him." (18: 103-105)

Accordingly, God (*SWT*) has commanded the true believers to avoid sitting and listening to those people who are indulged in denial and skeptical talks about Him and His Divine revelations:

وَإِذَا رَأَيْتَ ٱلَّذِينَ يَخُوضُونَ فِىٓ ءَايَـٰتِنَا فَأَعْرِضْ عَنْهُمْ حَتَّىٰ يَخُوضُواْ فِى حَدِيثٍ غَيْرِهِۦ وَإِمَّا يُنسِيَنَّكَ ٱلشَّيْطَـٰنُ فَلَا تَقْعُدْ بَعْدَ ٱلذِّكْرَىٰ مَعَ ٱلْقَوْمِ ٱلظَّـٰلِمِينَ

"When you come across people who speak with ridicule about Our revelations, turn away from them until they move onto another topic. If Satan should make you forget, then, when you have remembered, do not sit with those who are evil-doing folks."
(6:68)

وَقَدْ نَزَّلَ عَلَيْكُمْ فِى ٱلْكِتَـٰبِ أَنْ إِذَا سَمِعْتُمْ ءَايَـٰتِ ٱللَّهِ يُكْفَرُ بِهَا وَيُسْتَهْزَأُ بِهَا فَلَا تَقْعُدُواْ مَعَهُمْ حَتَّىٰ يَخُوضُواْ فِى حَدِيثٍ غَيْرِهِۦٓ إِنَّكُمْ إِذًا مِّثْلُهُمْ إِنَّ ٱللَّهَ جَامِعُ ٱلْمُنَـٰفِقِينَ وَٱلْكَـٰفِرِينَ فِى جَهَنَّمَ جَمِيعًا

98

"As He has already revealed to you (believers) in the Scripture, if you hear people denying and ridiculing God's revelations, do not sit with them unless they start to talk of other things, or else you yourselves will become like them. God will gather all the hypocrites and disbelievers together into Hell." (4:140)

2. Materialism

In this form of deviation from the Straight Path, there is a tendency to consider material possessions and physical comfort as more important, or to have a higher priority than religious and spiritual values [12]. This materialistic approach to life is strongly condemned in the Quran, as shown in the following example from surah *Al Takathur* as God (*SWT*) says:

أَلْهَىٰكُمُ ٱلتَّكَاثُرُ ﴿١﴾ حَتَّىٰ زُرْتُمُ ٱلْمَقَابِرَ ﴿٢﴾ كَلَّا سَوْفَ تَعْلَمُونَ ﴿٣﴾ ثُمَّ كَلَّا سَوْفَ تَعْلَمُونَ ﴿٤﴾ كَلَّا لَوْ تَعْلَمُونَ عِلْمَ ٱلْيَقِينِ ﴿٥﴾ لَتَرَوُنَّ ٱلْجَحِيمَ ﴿٦﴾ ثُمَّ لَتَرَوُنَّهَا عَيْنَ ٱلْيَقِينِ ﴿٧﴾ ثُمَّ لَتُسْئَلُنَّ يَوْمَئِذٍ عَنِ ٱلنَّعِيمِ ﴿٨﴾

"You are obsessed by greed for more and more (1). Until you go down to your grave (2). Nay, in time you will come to understand (3). And once again; Nay, in time you will come to understand (4). Nay, if you could but understand (it) with an understanding (born) of certainty (5). You would indeed, most surely, behold the blazing fire (of hell) (6). In the end, you would indeed, most surely, behold in with the eye of certainty (7). And on that Day you will, most surely, be called to account for (what you did with) the windfall of life (8)." (102: 1-8)

In the above surah, the word *"takathur"* means man's obsessive striving for more and more material goods, more and more luxury comforts, and greater power over his follow men or over nature, with unceasing technological progress. A passionate pursuit of such acts, to the exclusion of everything else, would certainly deviate man from God's Straight Path by disregarding His guidance, violating His moral codes, neglecting their obligations towards their fellow human beings, and getting indulged in the pleasures of his flesh and luxury possessions. Such excessive worldly life leads to gradual destruction of man's natural environment, imbalanced distribution of resources, as well as disgraceful life of frustration, confusion and unhappiness. Most importantly, on the Day of Judgment, people will be questioned about the pleasures of this world, how they acquired them? And what they did with them?

- Good deeds weight heavier than worldly adornments:

God (*SWT*) says in surah *"Al Kahf"*:

ٱلْمَالُ وَٱلْبَنُونَ زِينَةُ ٱلْحَيَوٰةِ ٱلدُّنْيَا ۖ وَٱلْبَٰقِيَٰتُ ٱلصَّٰلِحَٰتُ خَيْرٌ عِندَ رَبِّكَ ثَوَابًا وَخَيْرٌ أَمَلًا

"Wealth and children are the attractions of this worldly life, but lasting good works have a better ground for hope."
(18:46)

Wealth and children are the most important things people possess in this life. Islam does not forbid enjoying them, but rather it calls us to maintain a balance that keeps their appropriate values in relation to the everlasting life to come. They are adornments, but not criteria for people success in this life. True value should be given to what endures, and that mean all good works.

- Wealth and children distract man from remembrance of God and in giving charity:

God (*SWT*) says in surah *"Al Munafiqun"*:

يَٰأَيُّهَا ٱلَّذِينَ آمَنُوا لَا تُلْهِكُمْ أَمْوَٰلُكُمْ وَلَا أَوْلَٰدُكُمْ عَن ذِكْرِ ٱللَّهِ ۚ وَمَن يَفْعَلْ ذَٰلِكَ فَأُوْلَٰئِكَ هُمُ ٱلْخَٰسِرُونَ ﴿٩﴾ وَأَنفِقُوا مِن مَّا رَزَقْنَٰكُم مِّن قَبْلِ أَن يَأْتِىَ أَحَدَكُمُ ٱلْمَوْتُ فَيَقُولَ رَبِّ لَوْلَا أَخَّرْتَنِى إِلَىٰ أَجَلٍ قَرِيبٍ فَأَصَّدَّقَ وَأَكُن مِّنَ ٱلصَّٰلِحِينَ ﴿١٠﴾ وَلَن يُؤَخِّرَ ٱللَّهُ نَفْسًا إِذَا جَاءَ أَجَلُهَا ۚ وَٱللَّهُ خَبِيرٌ بِمَا تَعْمَلُونَ ﴿١١﴾

"O' you who believe! Do not let your wealth and your children distract you from remembering God: those who do so will be the ones who lose. And spend something (in charity) out of what We have provided for you, before death should come to one of you and he says: My Lord! If You would only reprieve me for a little while, I would give charity and become one of the righteous. God does not

pardon a soul when its appointed time has come; and God is fully aware of what you do." (63:9-11)

- Wealth and children are trials from God:

God (*SWT*) says in surah *"At-Taghabun"*

إِنَّمَآ أَمْوَ لُكُمْ وَأَوْلَـٰدُكُمْ فِتْنَةٌ ۚ وَٱللَّهُ عِندَهُۥٓ أَجْرٌ عَظِيمٌ ﴿١٥﴾ فَٱتَّقُواْ ٱللَّهَ مَا ٱسْتَطَعْتُمْ وَٱسْمَعُواْ وَأَطِيعُواْ وَأَنفِقُواْ خَيْرًا لِّأَنفُسِكُمْ ۗ وَمَن يُوقَ شُحَّ نَفْسِهِۦ فَأُوْلَـٰٓئِكَ هُمُ ٱلْمُفْلِحُونَ ﴿١٦﴾

"Your wealth and your children are only trials from God, whereas with God there is a great reward. Remain conscious of God as you can, listen to Him, obey Him, and spend in charity for your own good. Those who are saved from their own greediness will be the prosperous ones." (64:15-18)

3. Sectarianism

It is defined as an excessive, narrow minded devotion to a particular sect, especially in religion, that lead to prejudice, discrimination, malice, and violence towards members, or presumed members, of a religious sect.

A sect –or a denomination –is a division or grouping within a faith e.g. Sunni and Shia within Islam, Protestants and Catholics within Christianity, Orthodox and Reform within Judaism. Sects within one faith share the same fundamental elements of the faith but have different practices or different interpretations of specific elements of the faith.

The Sunni and Shia Muslims comprise the two main branches of Islam. The majority of the Muslims adhere to the Sunni branch, while 10 to 15 percent follow the Shia sect. These two branches were first formed soon after the death of Prophet Mohammed (*pbuh*) in 632 C.E. centering on a dispute over leadership succession. However, over time, political rift between the two sects broadened to include theological and differences in religious practices as well [13].

For generations religious communities generally lived in harmony with each other. But recently, a rising wave of extreme sectarian violence is sweeping the Islamic world, particularly in Iraq, Syria, Yamen, Bahrain, and Pakistan. It ranges from suicide bombing through terrorist attacks on innocent Muslims and non- Muslims. In fact, the mass slaughter of Muslims at the hands of extreme Islamic groups is unprecedented in modern Islamic history. Indeed, sectarianism is the most serious deviation from the Straight Path that the Muslim *Ummah* faces today, and it could lead to the destruction of the Muslim world.

The following are examples of Quranic verses that illustrate Islam's stance on sectarianism:

إِنَّ ٱلَّذِينَ فَرَّقُواْ دِينَهُمْ وَكَانُواْ شِيَعًا لَّسْتَ مِنْهُمْ فِى شَىْءٍ ۚ إِنَّمَآ أَمْرُهُمْ إِلَى ٱللَّهِ ثُمَّ يُنَبِّئُهُم بِمَا كَانُواْ يَفْعَلُونَ

"As for those who divide their religion and break up into sects,
you have no part in them in the least: their affair is with God:
He will in the end tell them the truth of all that
they did." (6:159)

إِنَّ هَٰذِهِ أُمَّتُكُمْ أُمَّةً وَٰحِدَةً وَأَنَا۠ رَبُّكُمْ فَٱعْبُدُونِ ﴿٩٢﴾ وَتَقَطَّعُوٓاْ أَمْرَهُم بَيْنَهُمْ ۖ كُلٌّ إِلَيْنَا رَٰجِعُونَ ﴿٩٣﴾

"(Believers), this is your community, one community, and I am
your Lord, so serve Me (alone). Men have torn their unity apart.
However, they will all return to Us."
(21:92-93)

وَإِنَّ هَٰذِهِ أُمَّتُكُمْ أُمَّةً وَٰحِدَةً وَأَنَا۠ رَبُّكُمْ فَٱتَّقُونِ ﴿٥٢﴾ فَتَقَطَّعُوٓاْ أَمْرَهُم بَيْنَهُمْ زُبُرًا ۖ كُلُّ حِزْبٍ بِمَا لَدَيْهِمْ فَرِحُونَ ﴿٥٣﴾

"(Messengers) this is your community, one community, and I am your Lord, then, be conscious of Me. But men have split their community into sects, each rejoicing in his own."* (23:52-54)

مُنِيبِينَ إِلَيْهِ وَٱتَّقُوهُ وَأَقِيمُوا ٱلصَّلَوٰةَ وَلَا تَكُونُوا مِنَ ٱلْمُشْرِكِينَ ﴿٣١﴾ مِنَ ٱلَّذِينَ فَرَّقُوا دِينَهُمْ وَكَانُوا شِيَعًا كُلُّ حِزْبٍ بِمَا لَدَيْهِمْ فَرِحُونَ ﴿٣٢﴾

"Turn to Him alone, all of you. Be conscious of Him; keep up the prayers to God, do not join those who divide their religion into sects, with each party rejoicing in his own." (30:31-32)

Repentance

Based on the Quran and the Sunnah, the word repentance (*Tawbah*) refers to the act of leaving what God prohibited and returning to what He has commanded. In other words, repentance is a process to correct any deviation from the Straight Path of a believer [23].

In the Quranic verse (66:8), the word "*tawbah*" has been associated with the word "*nasuh*" which means pure, sincere or genuine. Thus, "*tawbah nasuh*" implies sincere and faithful repentance. According to Islamic *Shari'ah*, a sincere *tawbah* is always accepted by God (*SWT*). It should be noted that repentance could not be accepted unless the nature of the sin (the evil deed) was known and was admitted by God' servant

Conditions for Repentance

1. Stop the sin
2. Regret deeply and truly for all committed sins
3. If the sin relates to the rights of another person, return the rights or the property that you unfairly took.
4. Make a firm resolution not to return to the sin in the future
5. Return to God for forgiveness of his sin.

Islamic Stance on Repentance

- **Repentance is to God alone**

Islam does not view any human being as infallible, i.e. perfect, flawless, or incapable of making mistakes. Thus, the only authority for the forgiveness of any human being is God, being the only perfect one. Accordingly, Muslims deny the authority of men to listen to another's person confessions and pronounce him forgiven. Regarding this issue, God (*SWT*) says in the Quran:

إِنَّ ٱلَّذِينَ تَدْعُونَ مِن دُونِ ٱللَّهِ عِبَادٌ أَمْثَالُكُمْ فَٱدْعُوهُمْ فَلْيَسْتَجِيبُواْ لَكُمْ إِن كُنتُمْ صَٰدِقِينَ

"All those whom you call upon beside God are but created beings like yourselves. So call upon them and let them answer your prayers – if you are truthful."
(7:194)

- **Believers should always seek repentance**

All human beings were created weak, and no one is free of faults and temptations. Thus, in the following verse, God (*SWT*) is calling all mankind to seek repentance:

وَتُوبُواْ إِلَى ٱللَّهِ جَمِيعًا أَيُّهَ ٱلْمُؤْمِنُونَ لَعَلَّكُمْ تُفْلِحُونَ

"And, O' you believers-all of you-turn unto God in repentance so that you might attain success." (24:31)

يَٰٓأَيُّهَا ٱلَّذِينَ ءَامَنُواْ تُوبُوٓاْ إِلَى ٱللَّهِ تَوْبَةً نَّصُوحًا عَسَىٰ رَبُّكُمْ أَن يُكَفِّرَ عَنكُمْ سَيِّـَٔاتِكُمْ وَيُدْخِلَكُمْ جَنَّٰتٍ تَجْرِى مِن تَحْتِهَا ٱلْأَنْهَٰرُ

"O' you who believe! Turn to God in sincere repentance. Your Lord my wipe out your
bad deeds for you and admit you into gardens graced with flowing streams" (66:8)

Even Prophet Muhammad (*pbuh*) used to say: "I turn unto Him in repentance a hundred times every day". Certainly, God loves those who turn much (to Him) and He loves those who cleanse themselves:

$$إِنَّ ٱللَّهَ يُحِبُّ ٱلتَّوَّٰبِينَ وَيُحِبُّ ٱلْمُتَطَهِّرِينَ$$

"Surely God loves those who turn unto Him in repentance,
and He loves those who keep themselves pure."
(2:222)

- **Forgivable evil deeds**

God forgives all sins and wrongdoings committed by a believer against himself or against others under the following conditions:

1) Those who committed shameful deeds against themselves and regret deeply and sincerely return to God for forgiveness and repentance: God (*SWT*) says:

$$قُلْ يَٰعِبَادِىَ ٱلَّذِينَ أَسْرَفُوا۟ عَلَىٰٓ أَنفُسِهِمْ لَا تَقْنَطُوا۟ مِن رَّحْمَةِ ٱللَّهِ ۚ$$
$$إِنَّ ٱللَّهَ يَغْفِرُ ٱلذُّنُوبَ جَمِيعًا ۚ إِنَّهُ هُوَ ٱلْغَفُورُ ٱلرَّحِيمُ$$

"Say: O' My servants, who have transgressed against
themselves! Do not despair of God's mercy,
God forgives all sins. He is truly the Most forgiving, the
Most Merciful." (39:53)

$$وَمَن يَعْمَلْ سُوٓءًا أَوْ يَظْلِمْ نَفْسَهُ ثُمَّ يَسْتَغْفِرِ ٱللَّهَ يَجِدِ ٱللَّهَ غَفُورًا رَّحِيمًا$$

"He who does evil, or otherwise sins against himself, and
thereafter asks for God' forgiveness, shall find God Most
Forgiving, Most Merciful." (4:110)

2) Those who did evil out of ignorance and repent soon afterwards. God (*SWT*) says:

$$كَتَبَ رَبُّكُمْ عَلَىٰ نَفْسِهِ ٱلرَّحْمَةَ ۖ أَنَّهُ مَنْ عَمِلَ مِنكُمْ سُوٓءًا بِجَهَٰلَةٍ ثُمَّ تَابَ$$
$$مِنۢ بَعْدِهِۦ وَأَصْلَحَ فَأَنَّهُۥ غَفُورٌ رَّحِيمٌ$$

*"Your Sustainer has willed upon Himself to be merciful so
that if any of you does a bad deed out of ignorance, and
thereafter repents and lives rightfully, God is Most forgiving
and Most Merciful." (6:54)*

إِنَّمَا ٱلتَّوۡبَةُ عَلَى ٱللَّهِ لِلَّذِينَ يَعۡمَلُونَ ٱلسُّوٓءَ بِجَهَٰلَةٍ ثُمَّ يَتُوبُونَ مِن قَرِيبٍ
فَأُوْلَٰٓئِكَ يَتُوبُ ٱللَّهُ عَلَيۡهِمۡ ۗ وَكَانَ ٱللَّهُ عَلِيمًا حَكِيمًا

*"God accepts only the repentance of those who do evil out of
ignorance and repent soon afterwards, those are the ones God will
forgive. He is All knowing, All wise."*
(4:17)

Summary

- The tenth commandment is described as the most comprehensive commandment, because it includes the entire moral values of Islam- its rightness or wrongness. God (*SWT*) is commanding the believers to follow these moral values because they are His Straight Path that would lead to happiness and success in this life and the Hereafter.
- The Straight Path is the path of God (*SWT*), the Prophets, the true believers, and the followers of God's commands. While there is only one Straight Path to God, there are multiples of ways that are distracting the believer and drifting him away from the Straight Path.
- Straightness means following the manners, the behaviors, and the conducts of God's Straight Path. This includes doing all what is right, whether committed, and to stay away from all what is prohibited, openly or secretly.
- Prophet Muhammad and his followers were commanded by God to stand firm on the straight path and correct any deviation that may encountered. This challenging task requires total attention

and continuous awareness of one's path through sincere prayers, soul searching, and choosing righteous companions.

- Among factors causing deviation from God's Straight Path are lack of determination, forgetfulness, hypocrisy, and satanic temptations. Forms of deviation in our time include intellectualism, materialism, and sectarianism.

- Deviations from God's Straight Path can be corrected through a process of sincere repentance. The Quran and Sunnah defined the guidelines and conditions for accepting or rejecting a believer's repentance.

References

1. Yusuf Ali, "The Holy Quran: Text, Translation and Commentary", Published in the USA by The Muslim Students Association of the United States and Canada (1975)
2. Sayyid A. Al Mawdudi, "Towards Understanding the Qur'an", translated and edited by Zafar I. Ansari, Published by the Islamic foundation, UK (1988)
3. Mohammad Pickthall, "The Holy Qur'an" (Translation and Transliteration), Published by the Burney Academy, Hyderabad, India (1981).
4. Muhammad T. Al-Hilali & Muhammad M. Khan, "The Noble Qur'an: English Translation of the Meanings and Commentary", Published by King Fahd Complex for the printing of the Holy Qur'an, Madinah, K.S.A. (1417 H)
5. Muhammad Assad, "The Message of the Qur'an", (Translation, Transliteration, and Explanations), Published by the Book Foundation, Bristol, England (2003).
6. Sayed Qutb, "In the Shade of the Qur'an", Translated and edited by Adil Salahi, Published by the Islamic Foundation, UK (2006).
7. M. A. S. Abdel Haleem, "The Qur'an: English Translation and Parallel Arabic Text", Oxford University Press, (2004).
8. "Definition of straight and narrow", www.thefreedictionary.com/straight+and+narrow
9. Mahmoud Shaltout, "Al-Wasaya Al-Ashr", Published in Arabic by Dar Al-Shorouk, Cairo, Egypt (1975).

10. Mohammad M. Al Sha'rawy, *Al Mushaf Al Gamie*, www.mushaf.com, Version 4.3 (2014), *Tafsir El Sha'rawy* for the Quranic verses: 6:151 -153.
11. Muhammad Rashid Rida, *"Tafsir al-Quran al-Hakim* (also known as *Tafsir al-Manar*), Dar Al-Ma'rifah, Beirut (1328 AH), Part 8, p.194.
12. CF. Ref. 9, p 9.
13. Cf. Ref 5, p.322, not # 80 – 81, and Ref. 2, Vol IV, p.118, note # 80.
14. Y. Al Quradhawi, *"Al-Khsais al-Ammah lil Islam"* (2001), Chapter 4, pp. 115-143.
15. Thameen Ushamam, "Is Islam a Religion of Moderation or Extremism? A Study of Key Islamic Teachings, Asian Social Science; Vol 10, No. 8 (2014), ISS 1911-2025.
16. "Definition of Straightness", www.thefreedictionary.com/sraightness.
17. "Standing firm in the path of Allah (*Istiqamah*)", www.rosetta-library.com/2010/06/24/standing-firm-in-the-path-of-allah-istiqamah
18. Ali Ibn Abdel Aziz Al-Ragehy, *"Al-Istiqamah*: its definition and importance", http://saaid.net/rasael/397.
19. Ibn Al Qay'yem Al Goziyah, *"Madareg Al Salikeen"*, Published by Maktabit Misr, Cairo, Egypt (2012), ‹Part 1, pp. 471-477 *manzalate Al-Istiqamah* (the place of straightness).
20. Naif Rashed Alrehili, "Intellectual Deviation: Concepts, Causes and Manifestations", DOI. 10.7763/IPEDR, 2014. V73.1 (Ministry of the Interior, Civil Defense, Kingdom of Saudi Arabia).
21. "Materialism" http://www.allaboutphilosophy.org/materialism.htm
22. "The World's Muslims: Unity and Diversity", Pew Research Center", www.pewforum.org/2012/08/09/the-worlds-muslim-unity-and-diversity-executive-sunnar
23. Cf. Ref. 19, Part 1, pp. 133-297 (*Al-Tawbah*)

Abbreviations

According to Islamic traditions, the following invocation
is applied when the name of God (*Allah*) is mentioned:
God (Glorified and Exalted, or)
(*Subhannaho Wa-Ttallah* in Arabic)
which is written abbreviated as
(*SWT*)

Also, every mention of the Prophet Muhammad* by name
or by title is followed by the following invocation:
Prophet Muhammad (Upon him blessing and peace, or)
(*alaihi-s-salatu wa-s-salam* in Arabic*)*
It is also sufficient to say:
"peace be upon him"
which is written abbreviated as:
(*pbuh*)

** This tradition is also applied to all other Prophets
and the Archangel Gabriel.*

Glossary of Arabic Terms

Allah   The Arabic proper name of the
                            One God, the Creator, and the
                            Lord of the Universes; the God
                            of Adam, Noah, Abraham,
                            Moses, Jesus, Muhammad and
                            all the prophets.

Amr   Order, command.

Faqih (pl. *fuqaha*)   Specialist in Islamic
                            jurisprudence.

Fiqh   The body of legal judgments,
                            opinions, rulings and other
                            works that make up a school of
                            Islamic jurisprudence.

Fatwa (pl. *fatawa*)   Legal opinion.

Hadith (pl. *hadiths*)   Sayings and teachings of
                            Prophet Muhammad (*pbuh*)
                            transmitted by a chain of
                            narrators.

Halal   Permitted

Haram   Forbidden

Islam   Complete submission to the
                            Will of God and obedience to
                            His Law and Commandments.

Kufr   Disbelief; covering the truth

Quran	The fundamental religious text of Islam, the direct revelation of God's message through the Angel Gabriel to Prophet Muhammad over a period of 23 years. As the literal and final word of God, Quran serves as the primary source of guidance for Muslims.
Shari'ah	The Islamic law, derived from the Quran, the Sunnah of Prophet Muhammad, and juristic reasoning efforts (*ijtihad*) in matters not specifically delineated in the other two sources.
Shirk	Partnership (Lit.); Polytheism
Sunnah	The "example" of the Prophet which covers his actions and statements and is a major source of Islamic law.
Tawheed	Monotheism, Oneness

About the Author

Hussein M. Naguib was born in Egypt and received B. Eng. in Metallurgy from Cairo University, and a Ph.D. degree in Materials Science from McMaster University, Ontario, Canada.

Dr. Naguib has more than thirty-five years of highly diversified technical and managerial experience in the semiconductor industry. He authored over fifty technical papers and granted fourteen US and Canadian patents in this field.

Since moving to North America in 1973, Dr. Naguib has been actively involved in Islamic educational and management activities. He was an Islamic school teacher in Ottawa Mosque-Ontario, Canada (1973-1982); a teacher, a management consultant, and Vice Chairman of the Board of the Islamic Center of Southern California-Los Angeles, CA (1983-1994); and one of the founding members, speaker, youth group teacher, and the Chairman of the Board of the Islamic Center of Temecula Valley -California (1996-2004).

Dr. Naguib retired in 2005 and has since dedicated himself to Islamic studies with a particular emphasis on analyzing and writing about the Quranic Ten Commandments, as the ethical foundations of a Muslim community in midstream.

www.ingramcontent.com/pod-product-compliance
Lightning Source LLC
Chambersburg PA
CBHW061744020426
42331CB00006B/1353